My Ego

MY HIGHER POWER, And I

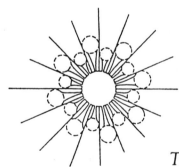

The ego is not all there is to us;
for deep within each of us,
beneath its thick outer covering,
lies the Eternal Truth which is God.

HI Productions
P.O. Box 7092
Van Nuys, California 91409

First Printing, October, 1985
Second Printing, October 1986
Third Pinting, October 1987
Manufactured in the United States of America
Cover design by Robert Howard, based on an original concept by Jerry Hirschfield.

ISBN 0-87418-014-7

Table of Contents

ACKNOWLEDGMENTS

I wish to express my deep gratitude to all the beautiful children of our Higher Power who have contributed to this book so generously — both those who gave knowingly and willingly, and those who were not consciously aware of their contribution.

A special thank you to my clients who have allowed me to witness and share in the dawning of their awareness of the Higher Power within their Being.

My deepest gratitude is reserved for the Higher Power within me who gave me the ideas for this book and who gently guided its preparation through often stiff resistance from my ego.

My ego deserves a vote of thanks also for finally recognizing the existence of a Power greater than itself, for becoming willing to surrender a little bit at a time to the Higher Power within, for gradually agreeing to give up its dogged insistence on controlling and managing and to accept the gentle and wiser guidance of the Higher Power for the common and individual Good of us all.

G.A.H.

PREFACE

The ideas for this book began arriving in my head in 1966 — long before I was aware that they were there or that I would some day be writing a book about them. They were vague at first, and fluid — not very cohesive. The initial seeds were planted by the people in the self- and mutual-help groups I began attending about that time. These people kept talking about the crazy things their egos did and how contrary that seemed to be to what their "Higher Power" wanted for them. After hearing these personal experiences and sharing my own for several years, I began to realize that I had an ego and a Higher. Power inside me like the people in these groups seemed to have. My ideas of what this ego is and what the Higher Power is began to solidify in my mind. The seeds were germinating.

Eight or nine years later, I realized that during the first 40 years of my present life, my ego had pretty much been in charge. I had been quite unaware of the Higher Power within me, and what's more, I didn't want to know. I thought that what I now call my ego was all there was to me. I was completely identified with it. I and my ego were one and the same. Whenever I didn't get what I wanted — which was quite often — I/my ego reacted with anger, resentment, disappointment, and hurt.

Of course, there were a lot of things I didn't like in my life. On the outside, everything seemed to be fine. I had a good job in an engineering management position which I had worked very hard for. I had a beautiful wife and two great children, a big house on a hill overlooking the San Fernando Valley of Los Angeles, a swimming pool, two cars, as well as a big backyard, two dogs, and two cats. According to the good old American dream, it seemed I had everything that should have made me happy, and yet, I wasn't. Inside me, something was awfully wrong, and for a long time, I didn't know what it was.

In 1969, a great change began to happen. Over the next year and a half, my "outer" trappings — all the things I depended on for security and "happiness" — began to fall apart. I suddenly lost my prestigious job; my wife contracted two severe illnesses and her death, or at least serious, permanent disability, looked like a real possibility for some time. I was sure we would have to sell our house to pay for hospital bills. I went into such a deep depression that my ability to provide financially became gravely impaired for close to a year. Looking back on it after these 15 years, it is becoming very clear that all those events were intended by that unseen "Higher Power" part of me to help my ego become aware of Its Presence within me and begin earnestly to search for Its guidance.

After the first several months of my depression, my sense of futility became more acute because I couldn't find a "position" in industry comparable to the one I had lost. Even if I had found one, I had severe doubts about my ability to perform in it; and even if I had the ability, I was significantly lacking in desire and full of fear. I really wanted out of my engineering management profession, but was too afraid to admit it or to face the imagined consequences of such a decision.

At the time of my deepest depression, my wife's illness became so compelling that I gave up all efforts at looking for a job and decided to devote myself to taking care of her well-being as well as that of our children and our household.

I believe that decision, which involved a long overdue, drastic revision of my priorities, was made for me in spite of myself. Another way of saying this is that the decision was made by the Higher Power within me rather than by my ego. As all decisions made by the Higher Power within us do, this one led to a series of miracles which I/my ego did not believe possible.

After several months, my wife began a slow recovery which lasted about two years. Today she is well. Although her diseases are incurable, they have been arrested and her symptoms have completely disappeared. I believe her recovery has been due, in large part, to her embracing a spiritual path similar to the one described in this book.

In addition, we did not lose our house, nor did we have to sell it at the time. After her recovery began, I was able to find consulting work over several years, which slowly led me into the entirely different profession I'm in today. The story of that transition is part of the series of miracles I mentioned above. It came about through an increasing awareness of the Higher Power within me and the consequent willingness of my ego to begin to surrender. It is too long a story to tell here, but it may be the subject of a future book. For reasons too complex to go into here, my wife and I separated seven years ago and divorced five years ago. We are now good friends and enjoy a warm relationship in which we share many of the ideas in this book.

In 1980, I was introduced to *A Course in Miracles,* a set of three volumes published by The Foundation for Inner Peace in Tiburon, California in 1975. When I first heard of the work, I was not overly excited. But my inner guidance kept gently urging me to pick it up and read it. At that time, I had already written several chapters of this book, and the ideas for the remainder of the book were continuing to take shape in my mind. Reading *A Course in Miracles* was for me a miracle in itself and another important step in my ongoing spiritual awakening. Here, in black and white, were ideas almost identical to the ones I had received, beautifully elaborated in a mystical, lyrical style.

My first ego reaction was, "My book's already been written — much better and more completely than I could ever do it!" At the same time that my spirit soared, my ego was disheartened and disappointed. I would have to start over and write another book. But the inner guidance from my Higher Power said otherwise. I kept hearing, "No, *A Course in Miracles* may be too large and too cumbersome for many people. There are those who may need a simpler introduction. Keep writing!" I did keep writing, and the result is the present book.

Though I speak of three "parts" of us in this book, I don't want to give you the impression that we are divided beings. We often appear split, and feel divided, isolated, and even alienated. That is only the result of believing too much in our ego, and therefore, not recognizing our inherent wholeness. The ego cannot conceive of our being whole. It cannot comprehend wholeness. Because of its linear, sequential nature, it can only concentrate on small pieces at a time. To derive a feeling of apparent comfort, it must divide, conquer, and control. Being whole, not only within ourselves, but also in the sense of being One with each other and with all Being is not within the ego's capability of comprehension and experience. Since many of us are still very much the apparent prisoners of our egos, we do not and cannot realize our Wholeness and Oneness which is the only Truth there is.

Speaking of the three parts of us is only a matter of convenience for communication purposes in terms the ego can understand. A highly enlightened Being once said: "I and the Father are One." If that is true for Him, it is true for every one of us because there is only One Father, One Collective Child, and One Truth for all. The Father and the Collective Child are indivisible, and I believe that ail the children making up the Collective Child are indivisible, whether our egos like it or not.

A Word about Pronouns

Since I began writing about 15 years ago, I have had difficulty with what has been called sexist language — using the pronouns "he," "him," and "his" to refer to a person, an individual, a child, a parent — also using "man" or "mankind" when referring to human beings or people of both sexes. In the late sixties and early seventies, the women's liberation movement brought this then-common usage to our attention as being unfair to women. Since that time, many organizations and institutions have published guidelines for non-sexist language, all of which have seemed to me very cumbersome circumventions. What everyone seems to be avoiding saying is that we need some new pronouns in the English language, which do not now exist.

In a previous book called *The Twelve Steps for Everyone . . . who really wants them,* I introduced two new pronouns to fill this need. I combined "he" and "she" into "hesh," pronounced "heesh" as in "leash." I also combined "his" and "her," and "him" and "her" into the single pronoun "hier" pronounced as in the word "skier," one who engages in the sport of skiing. These contractions of our existing pronouns seemed to fill the bill admirably. They are simple, do not introduce any new words since they combine existing words; and they are based on precedents already in use in our language, such as don't, can't, won't, wouldn't, we're, you're, and so forth.

Unfortunately, some people have had negative reactions to the introduction of these pronouns — to the point of not being able to read a book which otherwise might have helped them. Since the primary purpose of this book (and my previous one) is to help as many people as possible to become more aware of their true Inner Self, even if one person who might read this book were kept from doing so because of difficulty with new pronouns, it would be one too many. Judging by the reaction to the *Twelve Steps for Everyone . . .,* there would be quite a few more than one. My ego says: "Too bad for them; let them not read the book!" But the gentle, inner guidance from my Higher Power tells me otherwise, and whenever I can nowadays, I try to follow the Inner Guidance. I find my life much smoother that way — and many more people benefit.

So, in this book, you will sometimes find "he," sometimes "she," sometimes "he/she," and sometimes "he or she," or "she or he." In *The Twelve Steps for Everyone . . .,* I also used the new pronouns when referring to the Higher Power or God because I no longer believe God to be a "He" or "She," but an integration or combination of the two. Using the pronoun "Hesh" for God or the Higher Power helps me make the transition from thinking of God as a super-person or Super-Father as I did in my childhood to the new idea of God, as I understand "Hier" which is Infinite, Eternal Love, Beauty, Truth, Wisdom, Freedom, and Peace within each of us. Again, in the interest of being useful to more people, I have stayed with the more conventional pronouns for God as well.

I hope that in the future, the need for new pronouns in our language will be more widely recognized and accepted, and perhaps in a future book, it will be OK to use them. I would be glad to hear from any of you who would care to express an opinion on this matter. You may reach me at the address on the last page of the Epilogue to this book. Till then, let's all enjoy tradition!

G.A.H.
Sherman Oaks, California
April, 1985

INTRODUCTION

In my travels through this life in various capacities, I have been searching more or less constantly for a way to make sense of it all. Looking back on it now with a hindsight perspective, I can see that though much of it at the time seemed to be insane nonsense, there was under all the confusion, striving, wishing, hoping and dreaming an underlying reality that did make sense. Through some kind of process of elimination, I had to look in many places where the answer was not before I could turn to where the answer *is*. Many people on the path tried to tell me where to look; to guide me; show me shortcuts. Some of these people had an answer for them, for their time and place — others did not. At various times, I listened for a while, but the more they shouted, "Look here, this is the answer; I have it and I will give it or sell it to you; why look further?" the more I seemed to shy away and mistrust their cries. I could not take their word; I had to find out for myself.

Some of the people who tried to guide me in this way were parents, teachers, friends, supervisors in the work hierarchy, well-meaning relatives, people in various religious systems, psychologists and therapists, people in varous growth-oriented or encounter groups, and other authority figures through numerous self-help and other educational books.

Once in a while, I eagerly took the bait; I grabbed for what they had and hoped that would be "it," or at least that what they were offering would provide a shortcut to "it!" Sometimes, I held on longer than I should have for my own good, far beyond the point where I knew this was not the answer, or not enough of an answer — trapped by the hope that eventually, if I hung on long enough, the answer would be revealed. I was unwilling to abandon an investment of so much time, so much hope, so much of my life — unwilling to accept that perhaps this particular path had given me as much as it could, and it was time to move on.

Don Juan, in Carlos Castaneda's *Journey to Ixtlan*, says, "Choose a path with a heart." Many of the paths I chose did not have a heart, but at the time, I didn't know that's what I was searching for. Now, I believe I have found a path with a heart — perhaps because I have discovered my own heart in it. I can feel the love, the caring, and the giving of others on the same path, and more and more of all humankind. Through their love, I am learning to love.

Through this path during the last several years, I have become increasingly aware of three distinct parts of myself. Each of these parts seems to have autonomy; each is quite unique and each operates in my life quite differently. Many triads of this type have been proposed before. Examples are Freud's id, ego, and super-ego; T.A.'s Parent, Adult, and Child ego states; Carl Jung's subconscious, conscious, and superconscious; and even in religion, the Father, the Son, and the Holy Ghost or Holy Spirit.

The triad I have discovered is different from any of these, but overlaps some of them. This triple entity which is the subject of this book is also its title, "My Ego, My Higher Power, and I."

This triad belongs to the class which combines psychology and spirituality. Others in this class are that of Carl Jung already mentioned — subconscious, conscious, and superconscious — and the four-part division of Transpersonal Psychology: spiritual, intellectual, emotional and physical, in order of increasing energy density. The distinctive feature of the three-part division presented here is that it identifies more clearly the self-oriented mode of believing, thinking and living (our ego), and the spiritual mode of beliefs, thoughts and actions (the Higher Power within us); and it places the capacity and responsibility for choice squarely on each individual one of us (the "I").

In this book, I show how most of us have lived primarily in the ego mode and how, through such living, we have created a spiritual vacuum in our lives which accounts for the emptiness, loneliness, frustration, and perhaps utter despair that many of us feel, regardless of how many external achievements we may claim, how many material things we may have accumulated, or how many conquests, trophies or awards we may have won. I then show how, through developing our awareness of our spiritual dimension, the Higher Power within us, we often find what we have been seeking all along in the ego world: love, peace of mind, and a sense of community and co-creativity with our fellow human beings.

I want to share this bit of knowledge with you because a number of people have told me that it has helped them make better sense of their lives. It seems to help people to understand why they do the apparently senseless, often self-destructive things they do when their best intentions are quite opposite to their eventual behavior. I hope that this way of looking at ourselves may be of help to you also — not only as another way of better understanding how we function, but also as a means toward changing yourself to make better decisions in your life.

PART I

THE THREE PARTS

"There is an inner and an outer side to everything; and the quality of the superficial mind which causes it to fail in the attainment of Truth is its willingness to rest content with the outside only."

— Thomas Troward

Chapter 1
The Development of Ego

Most of us begin life unaware of who we are or even that we have an ego, and continue to live in that state of unawareness for a good portion of our lives — if not our entire lives. We are unaware that we have an ego because our ego seems to be all of us. We are ego-centered, ego-controlled, and ego-absorbed. We have nothing else to compare to. We cannot and do not see anything else. When we look at ourselves, we see our ego and we think, "This is me; this 'thing' that I see with and this 'thing' that I look at is all of me; me looking at me!"

At the very beginning of our lives, when we are babies, we may see a hand or a foot moving in front of our face. We don't know it's a hand or a foot or even that it's part of us. We just see something moving and we grab for it. We may also hear a baby crying. We don't know that it's a baby crying; we just hear the noise. We may not even know that we're doing the crying. Slowly, as we become more aware of our body sensations, we begin to feel something when we grab the hand or the foot, and begin to realize vaguely that the hand or foot must be part of us in some way. Similarly, we begin to associate the crying with an unpleasant sensation in our stomach which is alleviated when we are given a bottle or breast to suck on with milk in it to fill our stomach.

Our first experiences in this life come through our physical senses: sight, hearing, touch, taste, smell. These are the faculties of our bodies. We quickly learn to sense the environment around us and to interpret our sensations. We enjoy the feel of our bodies when being washed, changed, touched, held, or tickled. We dislike the sensation of a wet diaper, an empty stomach, or a gas bubble. Through these sensations and activities we learn about our bodies, and soon come to know ourselves as separate from mommy, daddy or other people. Separate bodies mean separate people. We, the "I" in us, become identified with the body. I am my body; you are your body. I am the body being held, touched, washed, dressed; you are the body doing the holding, touching, washing and dressing. Of course, I learn to touch also. I grasp your finger and hang on to it and play with it. Thus, you help me develop my sense of me as separate from you.

Even before knowing mommy as a complete body, I may learn to know her through the sense of being held against her warm, soft body, or as a smiling face uttering soothing noises while peering down into my crib, or as the hand held out toward me, whose finger I grasp.

By the time we are two or three, we have usually learned to speak, to feed ourselves to some degree, and in many cases we are toilet-trained. These are all functions carried out in the physical, space-time world under the direction of the ego which, without being aware of it, we identify with self. We have also been taught the meaning of mine and yours: my toys, your tools; my arm or leg versus yours. Our world is largely a world of objects, people, and locations or "people, places, and things." We know there is a place to sleep, a place to eat, a place or places to play, and a place to go to the bathroom. We have also learned that there are usually specific times at which these activities take place. There is a time when mommy or daddy goes away and a time when they come home again. By this time also, we have learned the meaning of "No." We have been told "No" many times when we wanted to go out of the house alone, play with our food instead of eating it, pick up and look at a delicate object, touch a hot stove, or climb on a chair or a table. So our world has also become one of yes's and no's. The yes's usually feel good and the no's usually feel bad. Perhaps we have learned through experience that touching a hot stove or a flame hurts, or that having our fingers slapped when picking up mommy's favorite flower vase doesn't feel good. We have also learned that having mommy or daddy close by does feel good and that certain foods — usually sweet — taste really good, whereas others taste rather bad.

So our world now includes good and bad categories, and most of our experiences are integrated either by ourselves or for us by adults as good or bad. We are good when we do what mommy or daddy or other adults tell us to, and we are bad when we don't. Even at this early age, we're rewarded for being or doing what someone else wants us to be or do, and we're often reprimanded when we tend to be our curious, creative, experimental selves, especially if it interferes with the wishes or goes against the directions of "grown-ups." Of course, this is all for our own safety and well-being, but our safety and well-being are often carried too far. We're often told by parents not to do things which are relatively harmless to ourselves but which might create or increase anxieties in our parents. So the world of good and bad, which eventually extends to right and wrong, is superimposed on the world of people, places, things, and times, thus becoming very much a part of us, of our repertoire for living, or rather of the repertoire of our ego. For many of us, our egos carry these early-learned habits of having someone tell us what to do and when to do it well into adult life.

Perhaps around the age of three or four, we're made aware of the existence of God — usually by parents teaching us to say a simple childhood prayer or perhaps by their taking us to church or temple. It is difficult for most of us at that age to understand why we are asking things of someone we cannot see, hear, touch or smell — someone who doesn't seem to exist at all, but at that age, we have a quite active imagination and we tend to trust mommy and daddy. So we take it on faith that God lives in Heaven which is way up in the sky and too far away to see — but that He* is so powerful and magical that He can see everyone and everything on earth. Most of us tend to make Him another daddy, which can be confusing, or perhaps a Superdaddy who is a daddy even to mommies and daddies. We might, of course, make Him or Her a Supermommy, but we are told that God is a "He" and He is always referred to as He, so most of us don't question that until much later — if ever.

Of course, we are told that God watches little girls and boys, and that He rewards those who are good and punishes those who are bad — a little bit the same concept as Santa Claus who brings us all those nice goodies every Christmas if we are good, and punishes us by not bringing any, or bringing less, if we're bad. God, we are told, does this watching on a constant basis and writes it all down in a big, black book. Since most of us are not saints, we grow up with a lot of guilt and fear associated with the idea of God. Some of us develop this negativism to such a point that we sort of shove God into a little corner of our awareness, hoping that if we don't pay too much attention to Him, He won't notice us. Others take an opposite tack, thinking that if we pray a lot and behave extremely well, God will be pleased or

* *As explained in the Preface, I consider God to be androgynous — including both sexes. In deference to tradition, however, I use the masculine gender almost exclusively in this book. Occasionally, I call God "She" or "He/She."*

appeased, and will reward us handsomely by giving us what we ask for. When we find that the rewards are not forthcoming as expected, or perhaps even that tragedy befalls us at times, we become very disillusioned and disappointed, and stop praying altogether. In the extreme, we may even become angry at God, believing that He is punishing us for being good. So we decide "What's the use? We might as well be bad; at least it seems to be more fun!"

Perhaps also, when around the age of six or seven, we discover to our great disappointment that Santa Claus "really" doesn't exist, we begin to wonder whether this God mommy and daddy told us about might be something they invented too. After all, if they lied to us about Santa, why not about God? I believe, that as much joy as it may bring, the Santa Claus myth can be very destructive to children. The time when they first find out the myth they have believed in with all their heart is not true may well be the first time for many children that they begin to doubt their parents. Their faith in mommy and daddy is shaken much more severely than most adults care to admit or to remember. In the young child's mind, mommy and daddy, and Santa and God may be associated to varying degrees since all four supposedly reward and punish. Neither God nor Santa are visible. Though in modern times, Santa has become more visible in department stores or shopping malls, he can seldom, if ever, be seen coming down the chimney to deliver the toys. So not only faith in mommy and daddy who have lied may be shaken, but faith in God as well. He may be just another story mommy and daddy have made up. Whatever the case, most of us seem to end up with mixed feelings about God which result from viewing Him through our ego-oriented glasses rather than as He/She truly is.

In many of our minds, these mixed feelings and negative attitudes — fear, guilt, distrust — become associated with all things we cannot see as well, such as dreams, fantasies or daydreams. We sometimes wake up in the middle of the night frightened to death by a nightmare. We cry or call mommy or daddy who come to comfort us and reassure us that "it was only a dream." No one is really chasing us; it was *just* an image in our head that has no real power over us. Though still frightened and unsure, we try to believe mommy and daddy that no one really wants to harm us. But even to this day, some parents still frighten their children into behaving as they would have them with stories or threats of bogey men and a punishing God. I was born in France and spent my early childhood there. I can still remember living in fear of "Pere Lustucru" who was supposedly hiding in the space in the walls where the wooden, roll-up blinds disappeared in the daytime. If I wasn't good, he was going to come out and take me away to the land of naughty children. And I had a pretty "modern-thinking" mother! Parents who tell their children such stories seldom realize the extent to which they are trying to control their impressionable children by fear as well as fostering negative attitudes toward the unseen.

How many times in our childhood we are told to stop dreaming or daydreaming and get busy. Children are very much in touch with the fantasy world. They love to play with imaginary playmates and invent stories that may regale or frighten them even though they know the stories are not "true." Such activities are often discouraged by parents who worry that their children may not develop a firm grasp on "reality" if allowed to concentrate even a little on fantasies and daydreams. Many parents also devalue these imaginary excursions, calling them idleness, laziness, or worse yet, by continually urging the child to keep active, keep busy, do his chores.

Even when fantasies are encouraged, it is often done with the help of "grim" fairy tales, full of ogres, goblins and witches who eat little chidren, fry them for breakfast, or at "best" lock them up in dark rooms or dungeons. It is surely no accident that one of the most famous writers of fairy tales was named Grimm. Although fairy tales embody the wisdom of the ages in the form of myths, many of them are cast in such frightening settings that they seem more appropriate for adults than for little children.

One outcome of all this is that many of us grow up with much fear of, and very negative attitudes toward anything we cannot see, feel, taste or touch. At best, we are vaguely distrustful of the unseen; at worst we are frightened to death of it. And most of us do not realize where these fears originated. For many of us, these fears of the unseen manifest as fear of the dark. Our feelings, even as adults, vary from mild discomfort to sheer panic when we are alone in a totally dark room, or perhaps even close our eyes in a crowded room. We may then feel and "see" all those goblins and witches we have tucked away inside us descend upon us.

Since we cannot see God or apprehend Him with our senses or even comprehend Him with our mind, we include Him in this area of distrust and fear. We automatically depend more on the material objects of the world as real and trustworthy — the opposite of the unseen. All of this reinforces our ego, the center within us which deals with the material world in terms of space, time and apparent solidity. Our ego looks out at the world which appears outside the windows that are our eyes and interprets what it sees there. It says "This is real and that is not real." It decides what looks good and what looks bad; what intends good toward us and what can potentially harm us. And it is very often wrong.

Chapter 2
This Thing Called Ego

Since our ego is the part of us that relates to the outside world, it is constantly reinforced by our society's outward orientation and emphasis on the material, physical, space-time world — the world we see in the light of day, touch, smell, hear, and taste. In school, we acquire knowledge from outside ourselves about the external world. We develop skills which are supposed to equip us to earn a living in what we are told is a tough, competitive world with a limited number of jobs. We learn to compete for grades, in sports, and socially for boy friends and girl friends. We are taught that it is important to be the smartest, prettiest, most manly or coolest. As teen-agers, we dare not be seen in school unless our shirts or pants display the latest "in" label, our hair is set in the currently "in" style, our shoes are the "right" type. We quickly learn and constantly keep up with what is "in" and what is "out," old, or passé. Our vocabulary must be the latest lest we be covertly ridiculed or overtly accused of not being "with it." We learn to hold in and hide anything that might be unique or different, and reveal only what we know to be acceptable in today's up-to-the-minute styles.

Above all, we want to be accepted by our peers. The fear of feeling rejected or ostracized is great, and is a direct result of a strong identification with our ego. This heavy emphasis on the externals and on competing to be the best separates us from each other. We outwardly try to hide our differences while inwardly accentuating them in negative, self-depreciating ways. If we excel, we are proud but may feel guilty. We may even try for mediocrity to avoid the guilt and feeling "different." But not allowing our best performance to emerge, we become afraid. Our true identity is lost in the crowd, and our ego fights harder to remain separate against all outward appearances of sameness. Our ego relentlessly drives us to conform while remaining the champion of separation and being terrified by it. It creates separation within apparent togetherness, and lives in terror of the consequent loneliness which results from its separation and from stifling our own individual uniqueness.

The ego says, "I am different; I am unique; I am special; there is no one like me," and it either takes pride in this difference or it is ashamed and despairs in it. For some of us, it keeps alternating between these two extremes. Our ego sees us as an individual, separate from all others and separate from the world. It knows nothing of any spiritual bond between human beings, or between humankind and nature — and what's more, our ego doesn't want to know. It secretly or unconsciously wants to be master of this one individual, or in the extreme, master of the world or the universe. Our ego doesn't seem to care what it masters as long as it is recognized as *the* Master. Failing that, it will go to the other extreme of lamenting its sorry state, feeling completely unworthy because it cannot master anything, and judging itself to be the worst human being on this earth. All of these characteristics of our ego are largely the results of our upbringing. They are directly passed on to us by parents, teachers, guardians and other adults who, we assume, "know better" than we do since we are *only* children. We pick up this ego orientation directly, as well as through the media of books, movies, magazines, and television. Where else are we to learn but from big people who have been here longer and are obviously more knowledgeable and wiser than we? At least, they talk better than we do; they know more words than we; and they answer many of our questions as if they know, even when they don't. How are we to know that these older, bigger, stronger people don't have any more real answers than we do?

Very few of us indeed are ever exposed to the source of knowledge within us — to our spirit or soul as a source of wisdom, or even to our intuition as a road to that Source. Quite the contrary; as we become young children, we are introduced to books and reading, and then school and teachers. They take over the role of knowledge suppliers from mommy, daddy and

TV. By this time, the child ego within us has developed to a considerable degree. Our sense of "I" and mine is strong and is almost completely identified with our ego since no one has probably shown us or led us to anything different in ourselves, either by communication or example.

Our contemporary schools are excellent institutions for strengthening our ego's hold on the material world and that world's hold on our ego. The primary focus of school is the acquisition of knowledge from the outside — teachers, books, museums, newspapers. No one during our twelve years of compulsory schooling ever tells us that we already have the Source of all knowledge within us, and that what we are learning externally is only that which has been transferred from other people's inner world to the external one. The emphasis is so much on learning what other people have said, written, or done that we soon come to believe that this is all the knowledge there is, and that new knowledge is constantly being "discovered" or "invented" by people much smarter and wiser than we.

The external emphasis is typical of the ego. It doesn't want to know about any other part of our psyche because such knowledge might imply loss of control — of which the ego is terrified. Believing that the ego is all there is of us except for our bodies, we eagerly fall in with the fare of school subjects, grades, tests, book reports, and homework offered to us by the educational establishment. Though inwardly, some of us may vaguely sense that much of this is manufactured nonsense and somehow "fake," we cannot go against the overwhelming majority who seem to take all of it so seriously. The pressures to conform to the prevailing ego-view are great. Most of us either conform or rebel. We become apathetic puppets and are rewarded for it, or aggressive delinquents for which we are punished.

In contrast to the five-days-a-week period we spend in school, the few hours a week spent in church listening to spiritual matters offer little compensation. That is especially so because the spiritual matter offered in most churches has been filtered through a wide variety of egos. Many of us find such conflicts there with the more apparently urgent material world that we stop really hearing, continue to go only because we feel we "should," or cease going altogether. We simply cannot fit the ideas and concepts of the spiritual into our material framework, because it seems too much like the Santa myths and fairy tales which turned out not to be "true."

It never seems to occur to us that perhaps we are trying to do it backwards. Perhaps it is the material world which needs to be fitted into a spiritual framework to make any sense at all. With the little exposure most of us get to spiritual matters during our early educational period, we cannot even form a concept into which to fit our material world — nor are we ever triggered to consider that this might be a desirable thing to do.

Nearly all the emphasis in schools, movies, TV is on the material, four-dimensional world. What we can see with our eyes is real — what we cannot see is unreal; it is magic, fantasy, frivolous, not serious and often frightening.

Time always seems of the essence. Our lives are governed by the clock. Most of us get up at the same time every day, eat our meals at nearly the same time, go to school, play, do homework and go to bed at night at the same time. If we do not have a daily routine, we feel uneasy, or in the extreme, highly anxious. We are often told that we are lazy, shiftless malingerers or ne'er-do-wells. Unless we stick to our time schedules, we will never amount to anything in life; we will have no discipline and we will eventually degenerate into something terrible. Our sense of ego-reality is definitely anchored to the clock — a human invention!

After all, don't airlines and railroads run by the clock? Don't businesses open at a certain time each day and close at another definite time? Don't we need time to schedule events to be attended by more than one person? Doesn't the earth rotate on its axis generating an endless series of days and nights which accumulate into a year each time the earth completes one rotation around the sun? Of course, time is of the essence! The ego and the material world could not function without it.

The ego is also terribly hungry for special attention. It prefers positive attention such as praise, approval or admiration from those people it considers "important": parents, teachers or other authority figures. But if positive attention seems too difficult to obtain, the ego reverts to any means necessary to obtain negative attention, such as reprimand, punishment, and in the extreme, even imprisonment. In school, we obtain this attention by excelling in school work, performing special tasks for the teacher, or by disrupting classes and becoming a nuisance.

During the teen-age years, the ego tries for the same attention within its own peer group. This is often done by performing extra-daring deeds, or becoming the class buffoon, always telling jokes to make our classmates laugh. If we are caught acting out this unruly behavior, so much the better because then, our ego has obtained the attention of classmates, teachers and perhaps even the school principal. What a trophy for our ego!

The ego's craving for attention — in this case, negative — is largely responsible for the increasing waves of crime and vandalism in our cities. The large numbers of people living in cities tend to strengthen the ego's need for attention since it is more difficult to obtain there. In a large group, the ego feels lost, shaken, and treated like an object or a number.

The same is true in large families. In a family with more than two or three children, it becomes difficult for each child's ego to receive the attention it craves. Children then seek attention elsewhere — positive or negative — or slowly starve emotionally for lack of it. The child's ego may feel itself undeserving of the attention it needs and it then becomes self-destructive through lack of self-esteem, self-effacement, and self-depreciation. The shy, withdrawn child who appears to shun attention rather than seek it, is probably more starved for it than the outgoing child who is always at the head of the class or the center of his peer group.

Most of us carry many of these ego-learned attitudes and tactics into adult life. The home or the work environment becomes the replacement for school, but the process remains the same: first, seek positive attention. If that doesn't work, seek negative attention, and if that doesn't work, retire into your ego shell and become starved, isolated, and self-destructive.

Throughout our lives, most of us attempt to get enough attention for our egos to keep them satisfied. But this is an impossible task because the ego is never satisfied. It always wants more, and eventually resorts to obsessions and addictions to get it. Many a drug user or alcoholic has started on the road to addiction as a result of this ego quest for special attention, or as a substitute for not getting enough of it. The same seems true of overeaters, compulsive workers, smokers, or anyone in the grips of a substitute substance or activity they tried to use to fill the attention void felt by the ego. Actually, even the special attention it seeks is, in large measure, a substitute for a conscious working awareness of our true spiritual connection with the universe and the Higher Power within us.

As the ego continues to grow throughout our lives, it forms a rather rigid structure of beliefs and concepts about the way life is. This structure or system of beliefs and concepts — some of it conscious while much of it is unconscious — determines how we see or perceive the world, ourselves, and other people. We see out there, or even within us, what the ego expects to see and find. If what we see or experience doesn't fit in with the ego's belief system about how the world is or how people behave, the ego will either distort the perception to make the new experience fit the established ego system, or the new experience, idea, or belief will be relegated to the unconscious ego realm without any conscious awareness of the repression, and often great denial of the existence of the repressed material within our psyche.

We need not go very far to find examples of this. If we believe, like a good Boy Scout, that we must be loyal, obedient, cheerful, kind, courteous, brave, clean, and reverent; and in fact, we have hostile feelings toward people, born of fear of being controlled, manipulated, or even annihilated, our ego will generally hide its hostility using one or more of the largely unconscious defense mechanisms which have been identified by psychologists. One of the most common is denial of the existing but unacceptable trait or characteristic: "I am *not* hostile!" which is often said in a hostile tone of voice. Another is projection of the rejected trait or characteristic onto another person, usually close to us: "Look at how hostile you are! Your hostility is so thick I could cut it with a knife," all the while not realizing that we are covering up our own hostility. Still another is completely covering up (suppressing) our own hostility under a veil of sweetness and honey, even to the point of calling everyone, including complete strangers, "honey" and "darling." Of course, when we resort to such unintentional subterfuge, we have no idea that we are often harboring unconscious hostility. Some of us use one of the many compulsive escape routes to avoid facing the truth about ourselves — such as alcohol, drugs, food, or becoming compulsive workers, thus robbing ourselves and our families of deep emotional closeness by losing ourselves in an ongoing stream of activities. Or, we may become physically ill, succumbing to a series of increasingly serious ailments which may eventually require hospitalization and a number of surgeries. These are but two examples of the lengths to which the ego will go to express an unacceptable negative trait in a more "acceptable" fashion.

Our ego is cunning, baffling, and powerful. It can and does cause cancer, heart failure, hardening of the arteries, high blood pressure, muscular distrophy or any of a myriad other ailments, some of which result in the death of the body. Left unchecked to its own devices, the ego will kill our body, which it knows to be the place that it is most closely associated with. Who but a mad person would destroy his or her closest associate? Yet the ego does just this in many instances. The premature cause of bodily death is often attributed to heart congestion, blot clot in the brain, lung failure, or numerous other physical problems, or even accident. Upon deeper exploration, it can usually be laid at the door of the ego's mistaken beliefs about life. Even old age as a cause of death can be laid at the door of the ego and its belief that old people become feeble and die. This has been implanted in all of us since childhood, and reinforced by the evidence of our own senses (the selection and interpretation of which, as we have seen, is determined by pre-existing ego beliefs). Medical science, which is an ego-dominated science, also teaches us that biological cells must decay periodically and that the production of new cells must slow down with old age. There is, of course, also a spiritual theory about why people's bodies die, which is very different from the physical/medical theory, and the truth is that no one really "knows" why people's bodies die. In the absence of knowledge, everyone is free to believe what is most comfortable for them, and we have an abundance of beliefs about what constitutes life and so-called death.

Harboring within us an ego which is trying to kill us while telling us to trust it because it knows what's best for us, creates a great deal of fear and confusion in most of us. When we don't recognize our ego as the *only* source of *all* our fears, we project these fears outward into the world, and strong anxiety arises in us about all those fearful things out there that we can't control. The ego tries to control everything to alleviate its fears and anxieties, but by attempting to control the uncontrollable, it only aggravates its own situation.

The ego uses every means possible to maintain control of us and the environment (people, places, things, and situations) around us. If it did not do that, its game would be exposed and we would cease believing it. We would recognize that our Higher, Wiser Power has the answers for us and that the ego is only trying to sell us a "bill of goods" to further its own purpose of absolute mastery over everything.

To maintain control, the ego must find scapegoats for the fears its impossible goals produce in us. It finds these scapegoats anywhere it can and convinces us that our fears are caused by these external factors: fear of war, fear of disease, fear of death, fear of not having enough materially, fear of being alone, or to reduce the scale a bit, fear of driving a car, fear of other cars, fear of crowds, fear of shopping in a supermarket, fear of heights, fear of being in small, enclosed spaces, fear of those who are different, and many, many more too numerous to list completely.

All these fears are outer projections of the ego's main and only fear; that of facing itself and finding out what it really is. The ego's prime fear is the fear of exposure because, once exposed, it begins to disintegrate. Its sick, deceptive games cannot stand the light of day. When light is shed on them, the games, deceptions, and lies perpetrated on us by our own ego begin to crumble. We begin slowly to realize that we have been duped by forces within ourselves, pressed into service by our own ego to further its own destructive purposes.

It should be said here that the ego does not mean to be so destructive. It rather intends to protect us, to fulfill our most noble goals, and to make all our fondest dreams come true. But it has absolutely no idea how to go about this, nor is it within its power to bring these fulfillments to us. These are all in our Higher Power's domain, not the ego's. When our ego tries to take our Higher Power's place, it can only knock itself out trying, but can never succeed. All its efforts are inverted and turn out to be destructive rather than helpful. It trips over its own feet, so to speak, and everything it touches eventually becomes destructive.

So the ego hides in the dark recesses of our mind and points the finger at everything and everyone outside itself — yes, even at God. It's all His fault, or their fault. They are the reason for our suffering. We are just poor, misunderstood, little victims trying to do our best.

Is it any wonder that with something like an ego in charge of everyone of us, the world is in such conflict? The ego thrives on conflict because conflict leads to eventual destruction which, at some point, becomes its hidden goal. Where there is no conflict, the ego creates it because that is all it knows. Conflict is its way of "life." Without conflict, there is no need for an ego. The ego really has no choice. Our belief in it gives it its power, and with this power, it must pursue its goal until all is destroyed.

If all this is true, how has the world survived to this date without being destroyed? Why has the ego power of all men and women not resulted in utter destruction? It is true it has resulted in a great deal of havoc, mayhem, murder, thievery, utterly desolate, destructive wars and all the suffering they entail. But somehow, in spite of all that, the world and most of the people in it survive; and its human population continues to grow. In the past 35 years, we have come dangerously close to destroying ourselves through a nuclear holocaust, and there are those who, today, believe this to be more possible than ever. But it has not happened yet, and we must pray and trust that sanity within our "leaders" and within ourselves will prevail over the forces of the ego so that it will not happen.

I believe the explanation of the riddle of survival is that there is in the universe and within each of us a Power greater than the ego, greater than the physical universe because It creates that universe, greater than any destructive force the ego can muster. This Power is the Creative Power of Love, of brotherhood, of unity and union, of sharing and caring. It is a Spiritual Power; the

Power and energy which we truly are, above and beyond and prior to anything physical we may manifest. It is the benevolent, creative, sustaining, loving, enabling, joyous, infinite, eternal Power many of us call God.

Being immersed, as most of us are, from the day of our birth in the world and power of the ego, it is extremely difficult for us to believe that such a magnificent, glorious, heartwarming Power can exist, let alone have anything to do with our personal lives. We seem to have to go to great lengths exhausting the power of our egos and suffering all the horrible consequences of that before we become willing to believe that perhaps there is a better way. Some alcoholics lie in the gutter face down, drunk in every bone in their body, unable to get up no matter how hard they try, and insist that their drinking is under control and they can handle it themselves. They are not yet ready to accept the help of a Power greater than their ego which keeps insisting "I can do it myself; I don't need any help." This is the ultimate in separation, the ultimate in "self-will run riot." And yet, at the same time, it is the moment which brings us to the point of surrender — where we become willing to believe that there may just be a better way — and we utter the words, "Please help me!"

It matters little what form the ego disease may take. When we substitute our own ego for God —

the Power greater than our ego — the result is always the same; we become insane or we die. The only way it seems we can avoid those painful outcomes is to reach a point of surrender and accept a Power greater than ourselves. It does not matter whether the symptom is alcohol, drugs, crime, neurosis, or any other addiction or compulsion. *The problem underlying them all is that we have allowed our egos to take control of our lives by ignoring our Higher Power too long.* And the cure is always the same — to surrender, to come to believe in a Power greater than ourselves, and to make a conscious decision to turn our ego's will and our lives over to that Power, as we understand It or Him or Her.

In spite of our ego's negative, destructive beliefs and behavior, we must not make the mistake of seeing the ego as a super-villain which must be smashed, killed, or otherwise done away with. Were we to attempt this, it would only be our ego setting up another conflict to be fought, another battle to be won. This is a natural reaction for many of us, as steeped as we are in the ego's ways. But the Higher Power's way is much gentler than that. It does not fight, kill, or smash anything. The Higher Power's way is the gentle way of Love. So we must learn more about this Higher Power within us, and more about the "I" within us who knows how to choose the way of the Higher Power over that of the ego.

As we grow in consciousness, old limits that we have allowed our egos to place upon us are gradually removed. We let go of old, false ideas thus making room for the new ideas of Truth to emerge. As we allow the Truth of the Higher Power into our lives — the only Truth there is — we no longer need our ego to be in control. We no longer need to protect ourselves because we learn to let go of fear and resentment. We learn that these are only manufactured by the ego. As we learn to love through a growing belief in the Higher Power, our ego learns to surrender and become a cooperative helper instead of a fear-ridden tyrant. Thus, we love our ego back to health so it can help us function in this four-dimensional space-time world in a sane and serene way.

As the title of this book indicates, I believe there are three entities or forces at work within us. One of these is the ego which we have been exploring in the last two chapters. Another is the Power greater than our ego, which many of us call God, and don't fully accept but perhaps recognize only in a remote way. The third entity or energy within us is what we call "I" when we speak of ourselves. I choose; I work; I play; I decide. Who is the "I" who speaks when we say these things? Many times, for many of us, the "I" is our ego. Certainly this is so when we say, "I fear; I attack; I defend." At other times, the "I" is our Higher Power as when we say, "I love; I care; I help; I join;

I unite with you." But there is another "I" which most of us don't realize exists. This "I" is our own individual expression of the Higher Power within us. This "I," the true "I," chooses, makes decisions, observes, picks one path over another. This "I" is always at work within us, sometimes consciously, but many more times unconsciously. At those times, we are not aware that we're making a choice. We believe we have no choice or the choice is being made for us. But even the choice to let another make a choice for us is a choice. Thus, we're always making choices, whether or not we care to believe it.

In the following chapters, we will examine the other two "parts" of us. Then, we will see how the three "parts" act and interact in our lives to produce the results we experience. We will also see how we can allow the true "I" within us to come more into conscious awareness so that we will be increasingly free to choose and to make wiser choices. We will learn to let our "I" help our ego to surrender evermore gently using the loving energy of the Higher Power within. Our "I" will transform the pain of ego bondage and resistance into the gifts of love, peace, freedom, and joy which the Higher Power within us is waiting to express through us.

Chapter 3
The Higher Power Within Us

Difficult as it may be to believe for ego-centered people like us, there is at the very core of our being, a Power, a spark, an energy which gives us life and which none of us can even begin to understand. Many of us tend to doubt or totally disbelieve this statement because it has not been scientifically or even theologically proven — or because we cannot see, feel, taste or hear this Power directly. Even those of us who accept the validity of this truth often have the attitude, "So what? So, there is this Power at the very core of my being. What's it got to do with what happens in my daily life?" We are not in conscious contact with this Power; we cannot see it, touch it, or understand it. Because of our ego training, we tend to disbelieve it or relegate it to the farthest corner of our awareness, if not discard it completely.

Most of us are not totally convinced that such a Power does not exist. Atheists excepted, we are afraid to discard it completely because we take some comfort in appealing to it in times of distress; and when we are desperate, it becomes absolutely essential. Furthermore, as we have seen, many of us associate our negative ego-oriented ideas about God with such a Power. We are afraid that if God is real and we do not believe, He will zap us or punish us in some way. We have seen how many of these negative ideas have been passed on to us in childhood. Because of these negative ideas from the past, we become very confused about God and this Power within us. Even such a venerable book as the Bible seems to tell us apparently conflicting things about God — so much so that innumerable religious sects have grown up around us — each with its own human interpretation of what the Bible says.

The Old Testament shows us a God of fear, wrath, and whim with immense power to destroy as well as to create. Creation of the Universe is, rightly it seems, attributed to God. But when God becomes displeased in the Good Book, He destroys or smites what He created as He did in the great flood, saving only Noah, his family and pairs of animals.

In the New Testament, Jesus speaks to us of an all-loving, all-merciful Father who forgives all sins and loves all his children equally, regardless of what misdeed they may have committed, so long as they are willing to change and follow Him spiritually. This is a little bit easier to accept and we can see some hope in this. But many religious interpretations of the New Testament still speak of good and evil, and a Judgment Day when God will tell us whether we are sheep or goats and dispose of us accordingly. It seems we are told to love God and fear God too — an impossibility, since love and fear are opposites. We cannot do both. Either God Loves us unconditionally and there is nothing to fear, or He loves us only when we're good and doing His will, but will punish us if we don't. It cannot be both ways.

An increasing number of people today who are growing and developing spiritually, are resolving the apparent conflict through a new belief in the great Truth that God is all-good, all-loving, all-sustaining and supporting, and at the same time, all-powerful and infinitely humble. This means that He will never use Power to control, to harm, or destroy anyone or anything — only to create, to build or extend Love to all who want it and are ready to receive it. Anything bad, evil, destructive comes from humanity who has wandered away from God and turned control over to the ego. In accord with this, is the belief that God doesn't judge, criticize, punish or condemn — only the ego does. God only loves, accepts, receives us with open arms when we are ready to say "No" to our ego and let ourselves experience God. In fact, God accepts us unconditionally and extends Love, protection and care to *all* of us at all times. But when we are under the control of our own ego or self-will, we cannot accept God's help. The ego is convinced it doesn't need God's help, or else, it wants to specify how God should help. It cannot and does not trust God to help in His own way.

That is why, according to this belief, so many of us turn to God only when we are in dire need and don't know where else to turn. Only at those times do our egos become willing to surrender enough of their imagined power and control for God's love to emerge within us. When we turn to God at those desperate times, He doesn't turn away and say to us, "Sorry, you have been a hypocrite because you only come to Me when you need Me." That's ego-talk. God always accepts us exactly as we are and welcomes us home whenever and wherever we return to Him.

Among those of us who are new to spiritual growth and just beginning to develop a conscious awareness of a Power greater than ourselves, a controversy often exists as to whether this Power, which most of us eventually come to call God, exists within us or outside ourselves. After we have been on a spiritual path for a while, this question disappears as we realize that the whole universe, including us is all One. It is all made of the same energy, the same spiritual stuff. All boundaries are artificial and recognized only by the ego. But at the beginning, this question is all-important because many of us don't know where to begin to look for God. We have all heard or read that the Kingdom of God is within, but we have also heard and seen God outside us — in majestic mountains, stirring sunsets, trees, plants or any of the beautiful manifestations of nature. We have seen God in a calf drinking from its mother's teat, a mother cat licking her kitten clean, or a tiny green shoot bashfully poking its fragile head through the sod into the light of day.

It seems much easier for most of us who are ego-controlled to see God outside of us. In that way, we can fool ourselves into thinking we are keeping God at bay. We need not let Him in too close. Our ego can remain "safe" in its illusion that it is totally in control of us. It can contemplate God's glorious works in nature for a while and then continue its ego-determined pursuits.

Seeing God outside us seems to be an intermediary step our egos need before they will allow themselves to contemplate and eventually believe that God may be inside or within us. As we have seen, this concept is extremely threatening to our ego. Believing that an all-loving, all-powerful Being is inside us and that this Power is more powerful than itself is just too frightening for the ego. Even if it could entertain such an idea, the ego could not comprehend it because it would expect anyone or anything so powerful to attack and overwhelm it. Since this is not happening, the ego concludes God cannot be inside us. It simply cannot understand or accept that God's Power — all powerful as it is — is *never* used to attack, but only to nurture, to help, to facilitate growth, to create, encourage, and sustain life. And this Power is within us, ready to be tapped and to manifest Itself through us when we become ready for It.

So the answer to the question as to whether God is inside or outside us is both. He is inside us as well as outside because God is pure Spirit, and Spirit is everywhere. Spiritually, there is no outside or inside. There is only One, united and indivisible. But to come into conscious contact with God in a way that will directly affect our lives, our feelings and attitudes, we need to learn to appreciate and come to know God within us. We can contemplate and enjoy the beauty of the ocean waves lapping up on the beach, the red and violet hues of the sunset, the bubbling brook, or the doe bounding through the forest, but all of these, as well as our physical selves are only outer manifestations of God who is inside all that we can see, hear, feel, or touch.

If we want God to guide us, which is the only way we will ever improve any situation in our lives in a lasting way, we need to learn to contact God within us. We need to learn to let Him or Her transform our ego from an insane, frightened, attacking, angry maniac to a more docile, accepting, reasonable part of ourselves which becomes more willing to step aside and let God guide us in the interest of self-unfoldment and wholeness. For many of us, this process of learning is extremely difficult and often painful, but it is also the most important thing we can do with our lives. It is our whole purpose for being here. We need to see it as most important and give it the highest priority if we wish to reduce our suffering and lead a joyous, peaceful life.

When we hear the phrase "God within us," many of us who are so materially oriented assume that it must mean "within our body." This is very confusing at first because we don't know whether God is within our head, brain, heart, liver, or where? No one ever seems to specify where within us He is. I believe no one specifies the location because God, being Infinite, cannot be confined to any particular place. He is everywhere at the same time. He is in everything physical and yet is more than physical. If this is true, to have God within us, we must be more than a physical body.

We have been told, too, that we have a mind and a soul — entities which are not easy to define. But since God is a Power, a Force, Energy, or Presence, perhaps that is where we should look rather than in our physical bodies. Psychologists have tried to define our minds, and philosophers to define our souls and they cannot seem to agree on a single definition. This lack of precision from the "experts" leads many of us to give up in despair. But perhaps, instead of giving up on ever finding God, what we need to give up is trying to define or locate Him, or even to understand Him with our finite, limited ego-minds — because we cannot. But we can experience God; we can come in contact with God and we can learn to see and accept His gifts in our lives. This is not easy for most of us ego-oriented people, but it can be done and is being done by many of us every day.

The Hindus have a good way of defining — or perhaps not defining — God in terms of what He is not instead of what He is. Because God is Infinite, our limited understanding cannot encompass all of Him. therefore, we cannot say what God is; we can only say what He is not. Any definition we can come up with cannot be God because, to be Infinite, He must be greater than that. God has no boundaries or limits of any kind, and therefore, cannot be defined. We know that He is not only the ocean, not only the mountains, not the sun, not the galaxies and not the Universe. God is greater than any of these and even greater than all of them put together. But we know that He/She is the Energy that created all of those and more, and that this creating Energy is still in every living thing and being, and always will be.

One of the ways we can come a little closer to this Infinite Energy is to still our bodies, still our minds, let our thoughts flow as they will without getting caught or attaching ourselves to them. We gently let ourselves go beyond all of these into the stillness that was before we and all of the universe were created. Out of the quiet void comes the still, small voice of God which we cannot hear amid the clamor and thunder of our ego. Of course, our ego, being no dummy, is fully aware of this, and that's why it keeps clamoring, thundering, demanding, complaining, feeling deprived or scared, getting angry, wanting more, and in general making a nuisance of itself under the guise of doing something important. Our ego cannot stand the stillness because that is where we consciously contact God. And when we come into contact with God, the ego ceases to exist as it has previously. It controls us with greater difficulty. The end of its destructive life is near. It can no longer function as the imagined supreme ruler of our being. Since that is intolerable to the ego, it will do all in its power to keep us from being quiet or meditating. In spite of the ego, though, all of us can and many of us have learned to meditate. It seems a long, slow learning process, but it can be done and is being done every day. By repeatedly asking the ego to be quiet as many times as necessary, we make room for God to enter (or to emerge into) our awareness. He cannot do this if we continually fill the spaces in our minds with thoughts, noise, or activities.

Many books have been written to teach us how to meditate. One that I particularly like is *From Intellect to Intuition* by Alice Bailey. This book covers the five stages of meditation very thoroughly and methodically. Jess Lair's book *I Don't Know Where I'm Going, But I sure Ain't Lost* has a very good chapter for beginning meditators, as does *The Twelve Steps for Everyone . . . who really wants them* (see Step Eleven.) We will explore the transformative role of meditation further in Chapter 13.

Another very good way to improve our conscious contact with God as we understand Him is to pray. Most of us do this when we're really in trouble. But what we need to do is to develop *an attitude of prayer*, which is nothing more than talking to God on a regular basis, especially when we're *not* in trouble. Many of us have strange attitudes *about* prayer that prevent us from developing an attitude *of* prayer. We need to learn to let go of the old ideas about prayer we acquired in childhood, and replace them with some new ones that work better for us and all concerned.

Our biggest stumbling blocks to consciously contacting God are the distorted beliefs about Him our egos have concocted or obtained from people in our environment. Many of us believe that God "only helps those who help themselves," and distort this into the fact that our ego has to be in charge for God to help us, or else we will just sit like bumps on a log waiting for God to do it all for us. This popular belief doesn't mean that we have to make all the decisions and take all the action. It means that we must become willing to do whatever our Inner Guidance tells us is God's will for us, realizing that this Guidance will never tell us to harm ourselves or anyone else. Others believe that God helps only the rich, the favored or those who are "chosen" in some way. What we fail to realize is that it is *our* ego beliefs that limit God. God, Himself, is unlimited.

God encompasses everything and everyone. He does not play favorites. He helps *all* of us alike and equally to the degree that we are ready to receive His help. God's laws are universal. They apply everywhere and to everyone without exception. Any thought of God choosing, judging, or helping only a select few is strictly made up by the ego. Most of us don't realize or accept these truths. Our egos would rather hang on to the belief that God is to blame for our misfortunes than to take responsibility for learning a new way of believing in and conceiving of God — a way which is closer to the Truth.

By hanging on to these old beliefs, our egos stop God's help from materializing in our lives. If we want all the unlimited abundance God has for each of us, we need to remove the limitations our egos are placing on God. We need to realize that many of our ego's conclusions and what we were told about God have been wrong. We need to make room in our minds and our hearts for what God really is — especially that He/She is within each and everyone of us and is at this very moment sustaining our lives, helping us to realize our Oneness with Him, and trying to teach us to love one another.

More recently in our lives, many of us have heard that it would greatly help us to learn to ask God, not for things or solutions to our problems, but only for knowledge of His will for us and the power to carry that out: "Thy will be done." When we first heard this, it seemed very strange and impossible. Our ego didn't want to hear about anyone's will for us, let alone carry it out. It wanted to continue carrying out its own will as it thought it always had. Or, if it hadn't because we had allowed another person or group to control us, our ego was anxious to get rid of this control so that it *could* carry out its own will (if it still had a will left to carry out): "I want to do what I want to do and nobody's going to stop me!"

So why should we pray to know God's will for us? When identified with our ego, we don't really want to do God's will anyway. We're afraid to know God's will for us because of the very limitations we have placed on God. We have seen that our ideas from the past are that God expects us to be "good" all the time, and will punish us if we aren't. And we know being "good" is no fun. We don't want any of that! Or, we think that being good all the time is too difficult. Only saints can do that, and we're certainly not saints.

If we become willing to see that we are the ones placing limitations on God, we can also become willing to let God remove these limitations. If we do this, our belief in God gradually changes. We begin to see Him as He truly is — all loving, helping, sustaining, nurturing, supporting, accepting, absolutely non-judgmental, non-condemning, non-punishing, and non-selective, loving each of us equally with a love so great that we cannot fully know it or imagine it. We begin to see that He is ever willing to help us realize our true closeness with Him, and willing to wait forever for us to do it, if necessary. For us, God is never controlling, pushing, or rushing; He is all-powerful and infinitely humble in the use of that power.

As our view of God changes in this way, we become more willing to ask what His will for us is, and for help in carrying it out. We come to know that His will for us is always beneficial to us, even if it hurts at times. We realize that only our ego hurts, and pain is often the road to the ego's surrender. God does not expect us to meet any expectations because He has none. He is completely accepting of us exactly as each one of us is at this very moment. Since He has no expectations, God will not punish us if we don't meet what He doesn't expect. On the contrary, since His Power is infinitely good, He always wants to give it all to us out of His infinite goodness. He knows the Truth that we are all His children created by Him, and as a loving Father would, He wants to and does give us everything He has and everything He *is*. We (our egos) are the ones who say, "No, that's too much; I don't deserve it." So the more we come to believe in an all-loving God, the more willing we become to know His will for us and to ask for the power to carry it out. We stop *telling* God what He should do for us while trying to disguise it to sound as if we are asking.

This old, limited view of God that we have is the ego's way of looking at God. The ego wants God to be limited, arbitrarily effective, and fear-inspiring, and we have bought that negative image hook, line, and sinker.

It is also difficult for us to believe that our Higher Power's will for us is the same as our will. We are so strongly identified with our egos most of the time that we have come to believe that our ego's will is our true will. We have become so used to this belief that we don't realize at all that although our ego wants to protect us and help us, the methods it uses are killing us. Our ego wants to have only fun, no pain; yet it creates pain. It wants only peace and fun. Everybody just go away and leave us alone; or else, make us the most special person on earth: the smartest, wisest, richest, most handsome or beautiful, most popular, etc. If you can't give us that, then go away and leave us alone. Little do we realize that if our ego's will were to come true, we would probably die of boredom or we would kill everybody, including ourselves.

Our Higher Power wants us to experience real joy or bliss, and to realize and accept our rightful place which He always keeps reserved for us within His all-encompassing Unity. It is right here for us to receive at all times. It has always been thus, and always will be. God wants us to grow and evolve so we may more fully express His infinite goodness, and be helpful for the good of all.

Another way which helps us to become more aware of our Higher Power's effect in our lives is to help another person without reservation and without fanfare. When our ego helps, it wants to get something back — something tangible. "What's in it for me?" Or it wants everyone to see the good we're doing so they will tell us and each other what a wonderful person we are; that we are doing so much good. But the God part of us just wants to help, period! He or She just goes about doing what can be done quietly, without anyone knowing. If anyone finds out and gives us acclaim, it detracts from the value of it just a bit. Our reward, in this instance, comes from experiencing the joy of giving or helping, and we find that when we don't expect to get anything back, we get back so much more than we give. This seems to be the way God works: quietly, unobtrusively, invisibly. The ways He does it are unseen. Only the results of His help are visible and these are often called miracles.

Because a part of us is God, miracles are not only possible for us; they are commonplace. It's not that we expect miracles from God in a demanding or complaining way. Rather, it's that miracles are natural for God and the God-part of us. They just happen — very naturally when our ego gets out of the way. A parking space opens up in a crowded parking lot just as we drive up, the right people for us come into our lives just at the time we need them, or if we humbly ask, and then release and do our "footwork," money arrives just in time to pay those ever present bills. The more we help each other in genuine sincerity, the more miracles happen in our lives and the more natural they become.

To allow God's help to work for us, though, we need to see more clearly how our ego is really sabotaging us, all the while feeding us a line of propaganda about how it's protecting us from attack. Our ego always perceives itself as attacked: "They're doing it to me; I'm just a helpless, innocent victim! My ego is OK; it's all those other people's egos I have to watch out for. If I'm not careful, they're gonna get me. I have to be on my guard 25 hours a day." That's how the ego tries to fool us and succeeds 98 percent of the time, unless we wake up and realize that is a pack of lies and there is a better way.

Since God is everything and unlimited, He is also our best friend. All we need do to have God as our best friend is to realize and believe that He is. Then, we can talk to Him as a friend. For many of us, the conversation may be a monologue because very few of us have ever heard God's voice actually reply — but the God inside us, the God we truly are, knows and hears and always replies, even though it may not be in words. A helpful idea comes seemingly from nowhere, or we actually hear words spoken in our minds which tell us to do something for our own good. If these words are also for the benefit of others, we can be sure they come from God. Of course, our ever-vigilant ego — always looking out for Number One — will often intercept these messages from the God within us, and we're off on another dialogue. But the voice of God is definitely there, within each of us. Let there be no doubt about that. The reason many of us don't hear it is that our ego is still so much in control that it won't allow us to hear it. We actually make an unconscious choice to listen to the stronger, more clamoring and more familiar voice of our ego because that is what we have always done. It seems sure and safe because it is familiar.

So we have to *learn* to talk to God and especially to *listen* to Him. We have to train ourselves to open the communication channel within all of us, between ourselves and our Higher Power or Higher Self. It is easy to start. All we need is a little willingness and a tiny bit of humility — just enough to be willing to believe that there is a part of us which is God and that perhaps that part of us knows better than our ego what is good for us.

We can begin by saying, "Hi, God, here I am —
one of Your children — and I want to talk with
You. I want to learn how to be in closer contact
with You as You exist within me, and I want to
know what You think is best for me to do." The
answer may come right away or it may take a long
time. Whichever it is for us, we need to learn to
accept it and continue to lead our daily life as best
we know how while carrying on our talks with
God and ever asking to know His will for us.

Some of us think that to contact the God within
us, we have to be very religious, read a lot of
prayer books, go to church or temple services
regularly, never say a four-letter word, and in
general, live the outer life of a devout or pious
person. If that works for you, fine. But it doesn't
have to be that way. It has been my experience and
that of countless others that we can contact God
whenever and wherever we wish because He is
within us and He is everywhere. Churches,
priests, ministers, and prayer books are there to
facilitate the process — to make it easier for us to
reach, sense, or find God. But if for you, these
don't prove to be helpful, they are certainly not a
requirement. This is certainly so if using these
means is only an outer gesture which takes the
place of the much harder work of searching
within. As always, it is the sincerity of the motive
behind the action which counts more than the
action itself. I believe God hears all those who
approach Him with sincerity and humility. He

even helps those who don't ask and don't approach Him, those whose egos are still too much in charge, but those people cannot hear Him and cannot accept His help until they are willing to surrender just a tiny bit of their ego — to make a conscious choice to stop listening to their egos exclusively and to allow a little bit of God's voice to enter their consciousness.

As we will see in Part II, coming to know the Higher Power within us is a process of coming to know ourselves as we truly are. After experiencing this process for a while, we come to realize that God is not a "person" — not a He or a She, but a Pure Spirit, the Energy of Life and Love and Unity within all. This Energy animates us, enables us to live as a spiritual/physical being, and gives us the power to love, create, build, and evolve. We come to see and sense God as a Presence, an Infinite Goodness, and we learn to express His Fullness through our lives. We realize the One God is all there is and He includes all of us and all that exists.

Chapter 4
"I"

We now have some idea of what the ego is and a bit of an idea about our Higher Power or God, and we have mentioned several times that we must and do consciously or unconsciously make a choice between the two. The third part of us in the title of this book, the "I," is the part of us that chooses. It is our will, the free will God has given us. It is the part of us that we are most unaware of, but our lack of awareness does not mean that it does not exist. It merely means that it operates unconsciously — out of our awareness — most of the time.

The "I" within us is also the center that observes. It does not make judgments of right or wrong; good or bad. It merely observes and records impartially everything that goes on, and then makes a choice between our ego and our Higher Power.

Actually, the "I" in each individual one of us is the expression of our Higher Power or God through us and as us. Since God is One and Infinite, He is all there is and includes all His creations. He has implanted Himself in each of us, and the part of us that is meant to express God in our own unique, individual way is the "I." Thus, the "I" is the individual expression of God in each of us.

When our ego is in charge, however, it doesn't work quite that way. Our ego often appears completely to overpower the I in us. Thus, the ego usurps the power of choice of the I. The ego goes to great lengths to assure that the I will remain its apparent captive, its tool or its slave, and will allow no choice to be made but its own. The ego wants to be all of us. It doesn't want to be bothered with an "I" that chooses or with a Higher Power that represents everything it is not. So the ego refuses to acknowledge "I" at all and tolerates some knowledge of God or a Higher Power because it is smart enough to know that if it protests too much, "I" will realize that something is fishy. Though it would dearly like to, the ego cannot deny all knowledge of God or a Higher Power. After all, some people have claimed the existence of God from time immemorial; a Bible has been written and does exist, and it talks a lot about God. So the ego does the next best thing that serves its interest of maintaining control. It relegates God to a position of relative unimportance. It invents a myriad of reasons why there is no God. Or, if there is a God, the ego claims that He certainly doesn't care about us. If He does care about us at all, He does not do so equally. God has His favorites — His chosen ones; as well as those He pays no attention to.

The ego points to all the pain suffering, killing, and selfishness in the world which it causes, and insists that if there were a God as powerful as people claim He is, He would not allow such things to happen. Very crafty this ego. It puts responsibility for the conflict, evil, and resulting pain of the world on God (or on other "bad" people) to ward the blame from itself, where the responsibility truly belongs, and we buy it! We (our egos) doubt God's existence and ignore completely the existence of the "I," our ability to choose. It is as if "I" were a prisoner of my ego, and that is precisely what compulsions, obsessions, and addictions are. The "I" has been imprisoned by the ego, which is now in charge, and drives relentlessly for ever-greater power, more complete domination and utter ego-centeredness of the universe. In this state, the free will that God has given us cannot be exercised. A free will requires a free "I" operating at the conscious level.

The "I" within us has also been called our consciousness or center of awareness. It is the part of us that is aware of being, existing; the part of us that experiences. Again, when the ego is in charge, and the "I" center has apparently abdicated its power of choice, "I" am aware only of my ego, believing that is all of me, and that the world created by egos represents all of reality. Fortunately, that is remote from the truth since "all" of me encompasses the other two "parts" of my being, my Higher Power, which is Inifinite, and I.

In this state of ego domination, the "I" appears to be dormant, but being pure Spirit, the "I" never sleeps. It only operates out of our awareness. Being of God, it must be true to the principle of free will. It can neither fight nor contend with the ego for the power of will. Fighting is not in its nature since that would destroy the Unity that is God, and that Unity cannot be destroyed. Since there is only One God who comprises all the "I's," the individual "I's" can neither fight amongst themselves, nor can they fight egos for power or control. All I's are unified in God. Therefore, they never fight. Thus, when the ego insists on being in control, the I, while apparently sleeping or being non-existent, is very much alive and doing the best possible thing. It allows the limited and often inverted power of the ego to play itself out destructively until the ego reaches the point of surrender, and becomes willing to learn a new way. Then, the I steps in and begins the reclamation job.

The "I" may be "awakened" from its seemingly dormant state in a number of ways. Its "awakening" requires first an awareness of a Power greater than ourselves within us. Without this awareness, the I cannot perform its major function since there is no choice to be made. The ego is in charge and making all decisions. But once we become aware of, and increasingly willing to believe in a Power greater than ourselves, which is within, we begin to realize that perhaps, even unbeknownst to us, we are making a choice. We can now choose to listen to and follow the domination of our ego, or we can choose to listen for and follow the guidance of our Higher Power: "Thy will be done, not mine."

As we begin to make these conscious choices, we realize more and more that we do have responsibility for our lives, and that through repeated use of our "I" to choose our Higher Power rather than our ego, we can affect the course of our lives as well as our character, personality, and attitudes.

Conscious, working awareness of a Higher Power, then, is a prerequisite to the development of the "I" to the point where it can freely exercise its function of choice. This conscious, working awareness may occur suddenly or develop gradually. It is quite different from the peripheral awareness most of us have. This peripheral awareness of a Higher Power lies on the outer borders or outskirts of our field of waking awareness which is normally dominated by the ego. This is the way the ego keeps God from working more fully in our lives. It relegates Him to the outskirts and keeps Him there. Its tools for doing this are doubts, fear of surrender, insisting that only what can be seen, heard, felt, or tasted has any real value. All of this is the direct opposite of the Truth.

For some people, this process of ego-control is reversed by a near-death experience, a sudden flash of revelation or illumination, an inspiration to perform a heroic act, or the witnessing of such an act performed by someone else. Our Higher Power is suddenly brought to our central attention and we come to believe that we are not alone.

More often, this awareness develops very slowly through ongoing interactions with another human being on a spiritual level, attending a number of meetings of spiritually oriented groups, repeated readings of spiritual literature, or by just looking deeply into ourselves with increasing honesty and humility. Meditation is a well-known method for awakening and developing our spiritual awareness, which has been practiced for thousands of years. A simple willingness to allow God to work in our lives without doubt or reservation is another.

Once the awareness of the Higher Power within us has been awakened, once it has come from a peripheral to a central place in our awareness, even for a brief instant, we are never the same as before. We have experienced a shift in consciousness which is the beginning of a spiritual awakening for us. We realize we are not alone, and never again feel that deep sense of loneliness which has plagued us for so long. No matter how much suffering we may go through, from that time on, we know it will pass; that it is temporary, and that at a very deep level, it is not real. Its apparent reality, as the reality of any pain or suffering, is only the reality the ego gives to it by believing in its necessity or inevitability. We no longer feel so stuck in our misery. We have had a glimpse of where we are going and we come to know that willingness, open-mindedness, and increasing self-honesty will help us continue to move toward our Higher Power.

As our awareness and concept of this greater Power within continue to grow, we find that at some point, our "I" begins to make conscious choices to seek and follow the guidance of this Power because we begin to trust and to know that this Power's intent for us is love and joy — that He has our well-being in "mind" and "heart." We become increasingly willing to make these choices and each time we do, the benevolent influence of our "I" grows a little stronger and that of our ego a little weaker. Since our "I" is our individual extension of God, its choices are always perfect. As our egos become more willing to accept these choices, the "I"'s perfection is increasingly manifested in our lives.

Our egos, being highly impatient, want to do all this perfectly, immediately — the right choice every time. If we remember that our ego has had years of training and habit-forming, while our "I" and our Higher Power were patiently waiting in the background, we realize that it may take some time for our ego to learn to accept those good, helpful choices made by our "I." After all, our ego will not relinquish control easily. Its inertia, which we often experience as fear, is too great. It needs time to learn and we have to help retrain it. Of course, the last thing the ego wants is to learn or be retrained. So "I" have to contend with an ego which thinks it knows everything and which has had years of self-training in being cunning, baffling, powerful, deceptive, and ruthless — all in the attempt to allay its fears by maintaining absolute control at all times. During these years, our ego has developed and refined all the techniques it needs to retain control, to keep "I" from coming to the center of our consciousness, and to keep us convinced that no one but it knows what's best for us.

It is amazing that against all these super-smart and super-critical ego forces, the "I" proceeds to come to the fore anyway. I believe this is because "I" am fed and fueled by the Infinite, Eternal Higher Power within us. That Power cannot be denied forever. The "I"'s mission is to perform the will of God — to wake us up to the existence of God, and to transform us from a mad, ego-dominated person to a calm, serene, joyous God-expressing being whose will is the same as that of the Higher Power — to unite with Him and realize our Oneness with Him.

It is helpful to remember that the emergence of the I does take place at its own pace no matter how much our ego would like to hinder it, eliminate it, or control it and rush it along. Part of the ego's cunning is that when it realizes that it is up against a Force greater than itself — especially a Force that will not come out and fight — it often appears to join that Force rather than fight it. In that case, we have the self-appointed preachers who tell us that only their way is right and we had better follow it or we will surely die in Hell; or in a milder way, the self righteous ones who gently tell us that only their path is right, and all others, therefore, must be wrong. In the extreme, this apparent joining of the ego with the Higher Power within us, which is really an apparent take-over of that Power by the ego, results in people who claim to be Jesus Christ or the Savior or Messiah. But this is just another ruse of the ego to attempt to control the Higher Power, which has backfired and gone out of control because that Power can never be controlled by anything. It can only be channeled through everyone of us who is ready for It in the service of the common good of all.

The "I" part of us has also been called the Holy Spirit — especially in both the old and the New Testaments of the Bible. In the Old Testament, it is often called the Divine Spirit. The Holy or Divine Spirit is the part of us that communicates with both the ego and the Higher Power. It is a part of God and is therefore One. It has been "sent" or established within us by God and is, therefore, individual within each of us. The Holy Spirit establishes a bridge between the Higher Power within us, which is One, and the ego which is many and separate. The Holy Spirit transforms all that the ego relinquishes into the Oneness, harmony, and love that is God. The individual part of the Holy Spirit within us, "I," accepts all the pain, suffering turmoil, conflict that the ego creates and eventually lays all of this at the door of the One Holy Spirit. The Holy Spirit converts this "mess" into the strength, courage, peace and love that we need for the work of transformation and growth. This is precisely the work of the "I" within us. As long as the "I" remains out of our awareness, the ego remains in control and plays havoc with our lives. We are hypnotized into believing that the ego and its world of fear and fight are real. We thus remain blind to the reality of God, which is the only reality there is since it encompasses everything — All there is.

As long as our ego remains in control, we suffer periodic or constant pain. We are confused, aimless, following meaningless goals, looking for answers outside ourselves, and eventually reaching desperation. The world seems upside down and backwards from the way it should be and we cannot understand why this is so. This is so because the ego is insane as is anything that attempts to live without God, and thus creates an insane world. The insanity, inhumanity and injustice we see in the world about us is but a reflection of the insanity of our own and others' egos.

At some point in this mad ego process, the ego becomes overwhelmed. Everything it has tried so hard to accomplish backfires. If the ego is ready to surrender, it cries for help. Even this little bit of surrender is enough for the "I" to "hear" and to begin the process of transformation from insanity to sanity, from conflict to peace, from pain to joy, from ego-domination to God-manifestation. The "I" goes to work immediately. Even before we are aware of the nature of our true "I," our "I" is already accomplishing its work of transformation. When this occurs, we experience a gleam of hope. We begin to feel that all is not lost; we are not alone.

To help the process along, we need to become consciously aware that we truly are this "I" so that when we are faced with the voice of our ego and the voice of our Higher Power "speaking" to us at the same time, "I" can learn to make a conscious choice to listen to and act only on the voice of my Higher Power, though still hearing and acknowledging the voice of the ego. So we can see our "I" as having two parts which are joined. One part is unified in God; it is the "I Am" that is God. Joined to this part and branching out from It are the individual "I"'s within each of us which are also in constant communication with our egos. This individual "I" is aware of everything the ego does although It does not interfere with it. This individual "I" is the part of us that receives all the hurt, pain, and fear that the ego eventually surrenders, and transforms it into something beautiful which is all a part of God can be. The individual "I" within the One "I" knows that the ego is not real. It knows that the ego appears real and passes itself off as real only because it believes in its own reality. My ego says: "I am real and all the pain that I suffer is real;" and millions of other separate egos cooperate in maintaining the illusion of reality for each other. At the same time, each ego vehemently denies that it's creating its own pain, holding other egos responsible for this. Thus, each ego locks itself into its own pain since it believes it can do nothing to end it. Each ego is thus reinforced by other egos in its belief in its own and other egos' reality, as well as in the reality of the pain which it believes is created by others.

But the individual "I" knows better. It knows that only God and His reality are real and that reality is serene, harmonious, loving and joyful. In (God's) reality, there is no pain, hurt, fear or suffering. The "I" transforms it all into joy and bliss when the ego becomes willing to surrender it. It is transformed from the agony of separation to the ecstasy of Oneness with God.

To maintain its apparent control, the ego clings desperately to the belief in its separateness and to the illusion that it can find a way to solve the problems and troubles it continually creates. The "I" knows this separateness is the ego's own illusory creation and reaches out to the ego waiting for its surrender of its own illusion. Since neither God nor the "I" are in any way controlling, managing, manipulating or pressuring, they will not interfere as long as the ego insists on maintaining its "I can do it myself" illusion of control and separation. They will merely wait for the first signs of surrender from the ego. Then the individual "I" immediately steps in to pick up the pieces of the ego's wreckage, and passes them on to the One "I" who transforms them into beauty and harmony so we can become the unified parts of God we have always been.

If the ego were to surrender completely instantly, the transformation from ego to God would be immediate and total. This seems possible in theory only. Theoretically, it would seem that since the One "I" knows no time, or IS for all eternity, it could work instantaneously, transforming all that is given It. The result would be a total and permanent spiritual awakening and transformation. The only limitation to the transformation process comes from the ego, not from God or the "I." Our egos, being reluctant and fearful of surrendering, let go only a little bit at a time, clinging tenaciously to every scrap of "authority" to maintain their hold on us. The transformation process, then, for most of us, proceeds slowly and gradually. But the important thing is that it does proceed. In Part II, we will explore some ways we can use to help it along.

Another interesting aspect of the "I" is that it appears to change as we grow spiritually. Before we have a spiritual awakening, which is the awakening of our awareness of the "I" within us, our "I" is completely eclipsed by our ego. The "I" always exists because it is a part of God and is eternal as God is, but it is as if in a sleep state where we are unaware of its presence. We see and know only ego. Since the ego sees everything backwards and inside out, it is really the ego that is asleep, while "I" is very much awake outside the ego's field of awareness.

In this pre-awakening period, when we say "I," we mean I, ego. I eat, I sleep, I work, at that time, is the same as my ego eats, sleeps and works. Once in a while, we may have glimpses of a reality beyond that of the ego, but we see it only as a pipe dream — something we desperately want to attain but despair that we never will. We just don't know the way; and if we are shown the way before we're ready to accept it (before our ego is ready to begin to surrender), it will have no meaning. We will dismiss it as nonsense, or as all right for "those people" but not applicable to me.

So during this ego-dominated period, when "I" and the Higher Power exist only outside our ego-centered consciousness, we are only ego. We believe no part of us can be a Higher Power, and we don't really know who we are. Who we think we are is *not* who we truly are. When we say, "I love you," we really mean ego loves you, which is impossible because the ego cannot love. It only appears to love and convinces itself that it loves, while it is forever looking to be loved. This is also impossible because no one can be loved until he or she truly loves. Being loved is a state which arises out of loving, and loving is a state of pure, unconditional giving in which we expect nothing in return because we need nothing in return. The only exception to this is when we are infants or young children, not yet old enough to give consciously. Even then, however, before our egos become fully developed, we give pleasure and joy to our parents from the Higher Power within us, through our "I," without being aware of it.

If we expect love from another, and bemoan the "fate" that no one loves us, it means only that we have not yet learned to love — we have not allowed our "I" to transmit the love of our Higher Power — no matter how much our ego may tell us that we are loving. What we are really doing is allowing our ego to shut off both our own love and that of other persons toward us. In this state of expectation which is a disguised form of demand, we cannot recognize or accept love from anyone, even when they truly love us. Love cannot be demanded. It can only be freely given and received. It cannot be forced; it can only be allowed to flow by removing the ego's blocks to it. It is the ultimate in giving.

The "I" within us always chooses the path of the Higher Power over that of the ego because it is the transformer, the healer, which connects us with the Holy (God) within us. As we pay more attention to our "I" and allow its choice-making power to assume greater influence in our lives, our limited consciousness begins to expand to come closer to the Infinite Consciousness of God. In that expansion process, our concept of "I" moves from total identification with ego toward the greater identification with the Higher Power. Eventually we reach that point where we have accepted enough humility to have some of our ego blocks removed. Then we can begin to realize our unity with God and accept our proper place within Him which He has always preserved for us.

There are no exceptions to this process. Every child of God will eventually accept his or her proper place within God until we recognize that we are all His children and we are all One. Every creature in the Universe is a child and a part of God, and therefore One with Him-Her.

Our "I" has also been called the Soul by past mystical and spiritual writers. This may be somewhat confusing. We all have heard of the Soul without having a clear idea of what it is; just as we don't have a clear idea of what God is. We have a vague notion that our soul somehow links us to God, that it is our essence, our deepest core. It is also the part of us that *knows* by intuition and telepathy rather than thinking or reasoning. Our soul is our "I" with a part of our ego attached. To grow beyond the limitations of its ego-part, it needs to learn many lessons. But it does not learn these lessons in the way that our ego thinks of as learning. Our usual ego learning is done by going to school, reading books, listening to those who "know" and taking in what they tell us. Our soul seems to learn in two ways: one is by direct connection with the Universal Soul which is God and knows all. The other is through the experience of our ego and physical body.

All our souls began as One, united and existing in God. At that point, "soul" and "I" were one and the same. But, taking "advantage" of the free will God gave each soul or "I," many of our souls created for themselves the illusion that they are separate from God, and thus willed to go their own way. As soon as a soul makes this decision to separate from God, he or she creates an ego to fill the gap between itself and God, and to try to take the place of God. As the separation continues, this ego becomes more and more powerful. It forms its own beliefs which are in opposition to God's because the soul has chosen not to live by God's principles. The soul then begins to pay more attention to the ego's beliefs than to the guidance of God, and it seems as though the ego has replaced God. Actually, nothing can ever replace God, but the ego believes that it can and that it does.

As a result of this process, it begins to appear as though the soul (including the "I") has been imprisoned by the ego, and the ego, "in fact," does act that way. It ceases to recognize God, Soul, or I as of any usefulness to its goals. Indeed, it sees them as hindrances.

While the ego goes its own unhappy way, thinking that happiness is just around the corner, the soul actually remains in the background. Though out of consciousness, the "I" and the soul are very much alive and active, always using the ego's experience for the soul's own learning and growth. The "I"-part of the soul is also guiding the ego as much as possible toward the experiences which will eventually help the soul learn its way back to God.

So one way the soul learns is by direct access to God, the Source and "Container" of all knowledge. But to the extent that this way is blocked by the ego, the soul uses and guides the ego's experiences to learn and "grow" its way back to complete unity with God. This is why, when we go through any experience, the ego sees it one way, and the soul another. The ego sees pain, suffering, vain attempts at control, and defeat; while the soul (or I) sees the blessing in disguise, an opportunity to grow, to learn, to expand.

When we surrender, our ego sees utter defeat and humiliation. Our soul sees a new beginning, a change in direction, and a smattering of humility. When we contract a severe illness, our ego sees only pain, immobility, inability to do the things we used to do when "well." Our soul sees an opportunity to rest, to change direction for the better, to learn to meditate, to learn the meaning of spiritual values, to develop new mental and spiritual faculties, which perhaps we were too "busy" to bother with while healthy.

When we think about death, our ego sees only the end of a lifetime, the inability to finish projects we started, the fearful unknown of what death is. Our soul knows that only the body "dies," that death is a transition out of the physical state to the spirit state, just as water changes from ice to vapor when the temperature rises. The ice dies and the vapor is born. Our soul knows that it may be a long way back to God because the only road is through the ego's surrender. Our soul patiently waits for the ego to stop the fighting and resisting which causes all its pain.

Chapter 5
Consciousness

Before going further, we need to say a few words about consciousness. Consciousness can be another vague, confusing term because it has been given so many meanings. It has been used to mean awareness, or an area of focus or concentration, or the scope or breadth of what we know and think about. Opposed to consciousness has been subconsciousness, meaning the things going on in our psyche of which we may not be aware or conscious; or unconsciousness which has been used interchangeably with subconsciousness, and also to mean the state of being passed out, knocked out or asleep. No wonder we're confused!

The following concept of consciousness has helped clarify the subject for me. I hope it will for you too. It is a rather limited concept since the subject of consciousness is so vast that it cannot be covered in one brief chapter. Volumes have been written on it, and more will undoubtetdly be written in the future. A much more detailed and comprehensive description may be found in Ken Wilber's *The Spectrum of Consciousness.*

I have come to believe that consciousness encompasses a spectrum somewhat analogous to the electromagnetic spectrum. This spectrum is a band of energy vibrations or "frequencies" (meaning rates of vibration) which vary all the way from zero (direct current) to infinity, which is obviously too high to measure with presently available instruments. On this spectrum of frequencies are located our ordinary house current which vibrates on and off 60 times each second, or 60 cycles per second; the frequencies our ears are tuned to (from 20 or 30 cycles per second to 15,000 or 20,000 cycles per second); the frequencies that carry our radio signals (approximately 500,000 cycles per second or 500 kilohertz* to about 1,650 kilohertz for the AM band, and 88 million cycles per second or 88 megahertz* to 108 megahertz for the FM band), and much higher frequencies for communication systems, radar, and the visible spectrum of light which our eyes can see. Above the light spectrum are X-rays, gamma rays, and other forms of cosmic radiation.

Each of these frequency bands requires a body organ such as the ear or the eye, or a technical instrument such as radio, a television set, or radar to detect or generate it. All are frequencies of electromagnetic energy vibrations, and all frequencies exist. But we can detect only certain bands of frequencies with our sense organs or instruments.

---

* *The prefix "kilo" means 1,000; the word "hertz" means cycle per second. The prefix "mega" means one million.*

In a similar way, consciousness seems to include a whole range of awareness, some of which we are very familiar with and some which we have not yet begun to discover. Unlike the electromagnetic spectrum, the consciousness spectrum appears to have no zero point where no consciousness exists. Some have called death a point of zero consciousness, but this is only the way it appears to the ego. We have long heard that the spirit within us is eternal. It has always "lived" and will always continue to live. We are seeing increasing evidence that the spiritual part of us lives on beyond the death of the body, and may eventually enter a new body at its physical birth, and live more than one life on this earth. If so, we need to move beyond the narrow confines of the ego which seems so strongly attached to the physical world, and find that there is no point where consciousness is not. There is only a point where it appears to the ego that there is no consciousness. This is similar to tuning a radio to any station on the dial. It appears that this is the only station transmitting. But move the tuning dial a bit to the left or right and other stations "come into being." The same can be said of radio and TV signals. To the radio, TV signals do not exist and to the TV set, radio signals don't exist. To our ears and eyes (without a radio or TV set) neither exists, when in fact, all are present in the space all around us as long as the radio and TV stations are broadcasting.

To the ego then, a "person" appears to be dead, to have no consciousness, when the body has stopped functioning. In actual fact, the consciousness of that person may simply have separated from the body and gone into the spirit environment. But from the point of view of the ego, death is total absence of consciousness.

Moving up the spectrum in the direction of increasing consciousness, the next stage may be a coma. A person in a coma is alive; the body is still functioning, perhaps with the aid of machines, but consciousness appears to be greatly limited, especially as observed by another person trying to communicate with the comatose one. The comatose person's consciousness appears to have left the body but may return at some indeterminate time.

A bit further up the consciousness scale, is the unconscious state where a person has passed out for one of several reasons such as emotional shock or a blow on the head. The sleeping state is very similar to this "passed out" state. Both are "unconscious" states. While asleep, we may dream, and that represents another step up the ladder of increasing consciousness. Upon awakening, we may or may not remember our dreams, or we may remember that we dreamt but not *what* we dreamt. If we do remember a dream, it is an example of bringing the product of one state of consciousness to another state where we may try to decipher its meaning or we may completely disregard it as jibberish.

The next step up is the daydream or fantasy where, even though awake, our consciousness is focused in a different place than our current physical surroundings. In a daydream our consciousness may wander aimlessly from one place/time to another without "conscious" direction, while in a fantasy, we are engaged in a more directed "waking dream" which may be based on a wish, a supposition, a replay of a past event, foreplay of an anticipated event, or an imagery or imaginary "trip."

The next increase in consciousness on our scale would no doubt lead us to what the ego calls full consciousness or the fully conscious or awake state. We must remember that we are looking at consciousness from the ego viewpoint because the fully spiritually awake state is much further up the scale from what the ego considers fully awake. From that spiritually enlightened state, the ego undoubtedly appears to be asleep, as it indeed is. But from the ego's viewpoint, we are fully awake when we are aware of ourselves, our bodies and the physical world around us, and we are able to communicate with each other through our senses. When in this state, we all agree with each other that we are fully awake, and thus define the fully awake state and the space/time reality that goes with it in this way.

But this is not the end of the spectrum. The ego would like it to be. It would like nothing to be higher or greater than itself and its level of consciousness. But the "I" or Soul and the Higher Power within us have other ideas. When the ego is at or near the surrender point, and becomes willing to admit that there is perhaps a consciousness greater than itself, the "I" and the Higher Power quietly make their presence known, and our consciousness enlarges a bit to the point where the ideas of something beyond our ego no longer seems so foreign or frightful. For some of us such a consciousness expansion may take the form of visions or hearing an inner voice, which has nothing to do with insanity as is often feared. It may be a feeling or sensing a Presence close to us or within us. Or, it may take the form of a transcendent experience — a first-hand experience of God. Many such instances are described in William James' classic book, *Varieties of Religious Experience.*

Meditation is an example of consciously bringing about an experience which transcends or goes beyond ordinary ego consciousness. When most of us begin to meditate, we spend a lot of time in ego consciousness (thinking) during the time we sit quietly and attempt to meditate. It is only very gradually, and with much resistance from the ego which keeps intruding, that consciousness begins to expand and to progress into the realm of experiencing the void beyond the ego. Many people's egos become very frightened when this first happens. The ego is so used to noise, chatter, thought, or talk that it cannot stand the silence of the void. It tries to fill that silence with every thought, judgment, and criticism it can muster, and we go back and forth between ego consciousness and God consciousness. As we continue to meditate, the initially very brief God-consciousness periods lengthen, and the mind which is enslaved by the ego, becomes calmer. At the same time, the "I" begins to take over any part of our will the ego releases. As this happens, we meditate more and think less. We become more comfortable with the emptiness which precedes and out of which arises the fullness of God.

Meditative states, visions, and other experiences of God are states of enlarging consciousness on the spectrum. Further up the scale are telepathic experiences and other psychic phenomena such as clairvoyance — seeing something which is happening in a distant place or in the past or future (pre-cognition), clairaudience — hearing something at a distance or from the past or future, various trance states such as those of Edgar Cayce or Jane Roberts, automatic writing such as that of Ruth Montgomery, or dictated writing such as that of Helen Schucman who gave us *A Course in Miracles.* Further along on the spectrum of consciousness are out-of-the-body experiences such as those reported by Robert Monroe in *Journeys Out of the Body.*

Some of these are difficult for the ego to acknowledge or comprehend because for many of our egos, such psychic phenomena or experiences do not fit within the framework of the way things are "supposed to be." Those whose egos are slightly more open, or perhaps a little more surrendered, do accept that such experiences may occur for some people, and are potentially possible for all, even though they may not have experienced them personally. This is really not too much different than people who are born blind, accepting that many people can see, even though they have never seen and cannot understand what "seeing through the eyes" means.

Some people among us are in touch with a consciousness much greater and a reality much different than that of the physical, space/time reality of the ego that most of us live in. The progress each individual human being seems to be searching for is the gradual transformation from an almost exclusive ego consciousness to an evermore God-like consciousness. This is an enlargement or growth process from narrow, restricted, biased consciousness to all-encompassing consciousness and love.

We now begin to realize that the spectrum has no end because, as consciousness continues to grow toward ever greater experience of God, it may eventually reach a point where all individual consciousnesses must unite and this union is God. Since God is Infinite, God's consciousness is the "end" of the spectrum. But this is not an end since Infinity goes on forever, and is therefore *endless.*

It may be helpful to realize that we all operate at many levels of consciousness simultaneously. The only part of our consciousness spectrum we are usually aware of, however, is the waking ego state. In our daily activities, we apparently go about making the necessary decisions of our lives using only the conscious part of our ego. We get up in the morning, take a shower, eat breakfast or not according to our lifestyle, choose the clothes we will wear that day, get dressed, perhaps put on makeup, brush our hair, go to work, and carry out the activities of the day. All the decisions required to accomplish those activities are conscious ego decisions made using our ego's will. While acting at this level of consciousness, we may also be aware of certain emotions. We may feel guilty or harassed because we lingered in bed too long. We may anticipate a difficult situation at work and experience anxiety while thinking about it. We may feel gladness or warmth as we anticipate having lunch with an old friend we haven't seen for a while. We operate at a thinking, feeling, and acting level simultaneously.

While we're doing all this, our ego is also invariably operating at a level of consciousness out of our ordinary waking awareness. Two primary activities of the ego are defending and censoring. It automatically and continually decides what is acceptable to enter our waking consciousness and filters out thoughts, feelings and actions that don't fit its image of ourselves. When such thoughts, feelings and actions occasionally do filter through the ego's unconscious barriers, they surprise us. We say, "That's not like me; I never do that!" or "Where did that thought come from?" or "Why am I so fearful? I have nothing to fear."

These surprise actions or reactions always come from a vast unconscious storehouse which the unconscious part of the ego keeps hidden from us so we don't have to face what doesn't fit our ego's image of ourselves. That image, which we often call self-concept, is who we *think* we are, or *should* be, or would like to be. Part of our self-image may be conscious and part may be unconscious. Some of it may match who we *really* are, but for most of us, a great deal of it doesn't match, and prevents us from truly knowing ourselves as we are. Further, these feelings and thoughts that our ego keeps hidden from us often make themselves felt through our body in the form of skin rashes, chronic headaches, stomach or intestinal cramps, colitis, or in the extreme, high blood pressure and heart overwork.

To the extent that our ego prevents feelings and emotions, as well as thoughts and beliefs from reaching our waking consciousness, to that extent, we do not know ourselves. We believe we are someone we're not, and don't know who we really are. It is a long, slow, and sometimes painful process for most of us to unravel the "snow-job" of our ego in our search for Truth and for ourselves — a process which is almost impossible to go through alone.

Our ego also operates out of our waking consciousness in another very subversive way, but a way which turns out to be helpful to our true purpose — the purpose of our "I." Our ego provides this help in a seeming roundabout way by sabotaging its own goals. At various points in our lives, we may choose some life goals. If our awareness of our Higher Power and our "I" is not yet developed, our ego is the part of us that makes these choices. The ego's goals may be a myriad of different things. Some examples are: "I want to get a college education;" "I want to be rich and famous;" "I want to be a manager or an executive;" "I want to help people;" "I want a close, intimate relationship with a warm, loving person." In choosing such goals, the ego generally isn't interested in any guidance from the Higher Power. Neither does it usually take into account our emotional readiness for the goals it chooses. Since the ego thinks it knows everything, it is not interested in learning. Since it is impatient, it wants to achieve the goal *now* or in very short order. Since it is flighty and fickle, it does not want to persevere for a reasonable length of time. Since it has a distorted image of our emotional development, it wants to know nothing of the hard emotional work required to undo the emotional damage we allowed to be done to us or did to ourselves in the past. Since it believes it is fully, emotionally mature, the ego is not interested in searching out the childish beliefs it still holds in the dark, hidden places of our unconscious. Even when they are discovered, the ego only lets go of these destructive beliefs as a last resort — when nothing else works. For now, the ego is interested only in achieving the goal immediately.

Because of this lack of preparation and unwillingness to put forth the necessary effort, we often fail to achieve the goals our ego sets for us. When we fail, our ego must immediately explain the failure in terms of something external that just didn't go right. "It's the breaks; I'm just unlucky. If it weren't for this or that person, I could have made it," and so on. If such failures are repeated, the ego runs out of excuses. At that point, it tends to conclude we are just failures; nothing we do will ever turn out right. It shifts the blame from the external world to us and concludes we are a terrible, incompetent, inadequate person and nothing can be done about it.

What is happening is that the ego, always thinking it knows best, sets itself up for failure. This is part of the destructiveness and insanity of the ego. It sets up a goal and consciously appears to do everything to achieve it, but unconsciously works against itself so that it will fail. One of the ways it does this is by wanting tremendously to achieve the goal, but without doing the necessary work. Consciously the ego says, "I want a close, warm relationship with a caring, loving person," while unconsciously it sneaks in with, "I'm going to overeat and be overweight so I won't look attractive to the person I want; I just can't help overeating." Or "Don't look at your fear of closeness which makes you push someone away when they get too close to you. Just ignore it and make it appear as though it's the other person who's afraid — not you."

After several failures, the ego says, "Stop looking. It's not worth the pain of continued looking and not finding; or thinking you have found someone, and then he or she turns out to be not 'right' after all." Until it feels really beaten and reaches a "bottom" through these defeats, the ego never seriously asks, "What am I doing or not doing, thinking, believing, consciously or unconsciously, to stop my good from coming to me?" or "What can I do or change *within* me to improve myself and my situation?" Honestly asking ourselves such questions is a sure sign of being at a bottom, and being willing to start up from there. Asking such questions is also the beginning of developing a new look at our failures to achieve our ego's goals.

As we become more aware of the Higher Power within us, we begin to realize that this Power is attempting to guide our lives through our souls which are part Spirit and part ego. The spirit part of our soul, our "I," knows that we're here in this life to learn certain lessons and build individual strength; and It knows what these lessons are. Possessing far greater wisdom than our egos, our "I"'s also know that the goals set up by our egos will not help us learn these lessons. In fact, satisfaction of our ego goals always delays our learning the true lessons our souls wish and need to learn. So our ego failures are always helpful to our continued growth toward discovering the Higher Power within us. Our souls learn more through the ego's failures than they do through its successes. This should not be interpreted to mean that our souls or God want our egos to fail, or that they want us to suffer. Rather, it means that when the ego sets goals which are counter to the soul's growth, and which the ego insists on achieving without the proper preparation, it is bound to fail. And when it does, the soul is one step closer to its liberation from the ego's domination. After a sufficient number of failures — different for each of us — the ego reaches a bottom and becomes more amenable to the guidance of the soul and the Higher Power.

For example, a person who is desperately searching for a close, intimate relationship and cannot seem to find one, always wants one only for ego reasons rather than motives of the soul. The ego unconsciously wants someone to lean on, someone to project its own negative attributes onto, someone to look after him and take care of him like a child. The soul, being wiser and older, may realize that he or she has not yet learned to grow up, to be a responsible, individual child of God, to be able to give and to receive. The soul knows that a relationship will not help the person develop these attributes because the ego's needs will feel temporarily satisfied, thus removing the incentive for growth. But the ego has to learn these things the "hard way."

If the person listens only to the ego, she may become bitter, self-reproaching, self-abasing.

Such a person may have perpetual anger and even rage against God, fate, or the Universe for not giving her a suitable mate. She may outwardly or inwardly complain about the unfairness of it all. If the person reaches a bottom and becomes more open to the inner guidance of God through her soul, she may choose to give up the search, remain without a partner for a while to build the strength of character needed to be an equal partner in a close relationship. When that happens, if she still wants a partner, the right one will appear without searching or effort. When our ego surrenders and becomes willing to cooperate with the soul in its growth, the people and things needed to facilitate that growth are provided by the Higher Power with little or no effort on our part. All of this seems like magic to the ego, but that is only because it is unwilling to recognize that anything worthwhile can be accomplished without great effort on its part. The Truth is that when ego barriers are removed through surrender, the Higher Power within provides everything that is needed for our well-being, and it manifests in our lives. If that seems to be magic to the ego, it is a very natural matter of course to the Higher Power within us.

PART II

THE PATH OF TRANSFORMATION

To trust in the law of good is to constantly believe that we are surrounded by a Power which can and will cast all fear from our minds, free us from all bondage, and set us safe and satisfied in a new order of living.

— Ernest Holmes

Chapter 6
Before the Beginning

To progress from ego to Higher Power by means of I, most of us travel different paths because we start from different places. I no longer have any doubt that our egos are insane, but they are insane in different ways. Some of us are only slightly neurotic; others have frequent psychotic episodes. Some of us suffer deep depressions; others over-elation, and still others flip back and forth between the two. Some of us frequently contemplate suicide; others would never dream of such a thing — yet they linger in an unhappy state, not knowing the cause or what to do about it. Many of us suffer from compulsions and obsessions of all kinds. We talk too much or not enough, we overeat, undereat, overdrink, overwork, and over- or undersex. We do things destructive to our bodies and minds such as smoke tobacco or marijuana, take in too much sugar, or take all manner of pills in an attempt to control physical and emotional illnesses which have their origin in our spiritual starvation caused by our separation from God at the conscious level.

Some of us are in a state of constant emotional turmoil; others would not know an emotion if they met one on the street, let alone felt one. All of these are symptoms or signals of deeper-seated problems or perhaps one deeper-seated problem:

too much ego control and little or no conscious awareness and contact with the Higher Power within us. Regardless of where we are, if we wish to experience any kind of sanity, stability, or happiness, we all need to progress out of our ego toward our Higher Power. We all seem to be looking for God and most of us don't know it, and would not believe it if someone told us that is our problem, as I'm telling you now. If we do believe it, many of us are at a loss as to how to proceed, where to begin.

Before the beginning, then, we are in a state of almost complete ego control. Some of us are in deep pain because we are constantly fighting our egos, knowing that something is wrong, but not knowing what, or what to do about it. We constantly search for a way out. We try all forms of therapy, seminars, books, religion, and even cults and so-called "pop" or brief therapies. If we are not yet ready to face the problem, we try more destructive escape routes such as alcohol, drugs, sex, food, overwork, physical illness, surgeries, not realizing that the route or substance we hope will save us, will eventually destroy us because we become addicted to it. We become addicted to and eventually obsessed with *anything* we use as a substitute for God. These means or substances become our idols and we become their slaves until we are ready to die or stop using substitutes.

The really self-destructive people who are so controlled by their egos that they have not even an inkling of what is going on — nor do they ever want to find out — may never come out of it in this lifetime. Indeed, their egos may kill their bodies before they have a chance to learn the true way out. Many bodies have died of illnesses caused by their own or others' egos. Some of these people are psychopaths and sociopaths. Some are in prison or psychiatric hospitals; others are free and walking among us. Every once in a while, one of these extreme, ego-controlled people succeeds in hypnotizing a whole nation into being insane with him. This is what Hitler did in Germany for twelve years, resulting in killing and destruction on a scale so huge it is difficult to comprehend.

Most of us are not nearly so obviously destructive to so many people when in the clutches of our egos, but directly or indirectly, we are extremely destructive to ourselves and to those close to us. Whenever we don't see and use our God-given capacities to the best of our ability, we are destructive. Whenever we insist on continuing our insane, ego-driven life without paying attention to our inner Divine Guidance, which is always available from the Higher Power within, we are being destructive. All we need do is turn away from the external idols, substances, practices, and people our ego constantly points to as the road to salvation, and turn inward toward the guidance from the Higher Power within us. As soon as we do this, the destruction stops and life begins.

We don't know this when we're under full ego control. We may not even know or acknowledge that there is anything inside us except a mind, a brain, and a bunch of flesh and bones, or plumbing, as some have called it. We may have very negative attitudes toward God, as I had, and want to have nothing to do with any Deity. We may become angry or afraid at the very mention of the word "God." We may not believe there is a God because if there were, we would certainly expect Him to take better care of us and the world than He apparently does. How can He allow the suffering to go on — even letting innocent little children be killed? Even if we do believe there is a God, we don't think He has anything to give us because we feel we don't deserve it. Somewhere deep inside us, we ego-driven people feel we're bad; we have "sinned" and continue to sin. Our insane egos invent all kinds of *reasons* why God behaves as *we* think He does. Our egos cannot conceive of the fact that they understand nothing; they know nothing; they are nothing. The ego knows only what it creates and calls it truth. But in fact, it is all lies because the ego is insanely destructive and knows only how to manufacture lies to maintain the lies it has manufactured previously.

We are so mesmerized, so enthralled by the false marvels of the ego and the world it has constructed, that we would rather doubt God than our own ego. We would rather believe the lies of our ego than the only Truth there is — the Eternal Truth of God.

So we continue in the grip of our ego, blaming, judging, condemning, pointing the finger at all the trouble the world causes us — not realizing that as long as we do this, we perpetuate our misery. Some of us feel terribly guilty that our lives are not smoother; others are full of self-pity. Some strike out in rage at anyone who comes near them, while others contain their rage, becoming deeply depressed and withdrawn from the world. In their self-imposed isolation, they get worse rather than better.

When we are in these depths of despair, which is where ego control invariably leads us, we almost always have extremely low self-esteem. We place very little value on ourselves; we feel worthless. Our egos have manufactured this condition, all the time acting as if they (we) were in control of the situation, as our ship was sinking. In some of us, our egos completely deny this condition and cover it up with frantic activity, fake enthusiasm, manufactured zest for life, and a false belief that everything is fine and that we are happy. Along with this denial, the ego often has to narrow down its sphere of activity while engaging more and more fervently in the one chosen activity where it's fairly sure it will succeed, to the exclusion of all others where there's a risk of failure. An example of this is the way I was headed — concentrating more and more of my energy on work where the rewards were tangible in terms of money and prestige, but narrowing severely my social activities and close contact with my family, where the emotional risks were too great. Another example which I also acted out at a point in my life is that of the perennial student who continues to go to school, taking courses compulsively because school is a safer and more protected environment than the working world. The usual rationalization our ego gives us for this is, "When I finish this next course, or get this degree, I'll be better equipped for more responsibility on the job, and then I'll get a raise or a promotion." But often, the end of the course doesn't come because we drop out in the middle, or maybe just before the crucial final exam. If we do finish the course, "There's just one more course I need after this one," and so on. You know all the "good reasons" our ego gives us to stay protected and safe, and appear to be in control.

For those of us whose egos don't take this path of denial, we fall into helplessness sooner. We think the whole world is against us and is out to do us in. We become angry or depressed or alternate between the two. We build up a tremendously negative attitude toward both ourselves and the world. We blame the world or society for not welcoming us with open arms, not recognizing our talents and our worth, for not giving us life on a silver platter. We blame ourselves for not being better, stronger, more capable, more like someone else to whom we endlessly compare ourselves, and usually feel worse than. Sometimes we feel like the whole world out there is "normal" except us. We're different, we're worse than anyone else. The longer we struggle with these negative ideas of our egos, the stronger they become and the more worthless we feel. At times, we reach the point where we think of committing suicide but many of us don't even want to do that for ourselves (thank God). We want God to take us and are angry at Him for not doing it and allowing us to suffer like this. We (our egos) can see no end to the suffering. We feel it will go on forever; so what's the use of going on?

Often long before we reach this point, we realize something is wrong. Messages from the "I" within us, at the prompting of our Higher Power, begin to reach through the ego's barriers. The messages may be in forms that the ego will be forced to look at, such as severe headaches, a spastic colon, skin erruptions, fainting spells; or they may be more severe ailments such as a heart attack, cancer, or a disabled organ which requires surgery. We may also have a series of accidents in which we are temporarily or permanently maimed or disabled. Many of us often go to doctors for months or even years, taking the pills they prescribe for our ailments, or undergoing surgery after surgery, before we are finally ready to admit that our physical ailments or accidents may originate from an emotional distortion caused by a lack of spiritual awareness.

If we do recognize that we have emotional problems which may be causing our physical problems, many of us often seek help through psychotherapy. We may go to an individual therapist, a marriage and family counselor, a psychologist or psychiatrist. But our ego is cunning, baffling, and powerful. It often tells us that therapy doesn't work. You just talk to this person week after week, and nothing happens; or progress is too slow and too expensive. Many of us think nothing of spending thousands of dollars a year on liquor, cigarettes, pills, doctor bills, or even new cars and other ego gratification "gadgets," but to spend two or three thousand dollars on ourselves as an investment in our emotional well-being, our ego thinks is just too much! It invents all kinds of reasons why we should not continue therapy, and we often quit after a few weeks or months without giving ourselves a chance to go into any depth where the real ego barriers are.

The ego also tells us, "This therapist is no good. He or she isn't making me any better. I'm getting worse rather than improving. I'll quit and try another one." Some of us jump from one therapist to another, spending a few weeks, or two or three months with each, each time repeating much of the same material and never allowing ourselves to work in depth with any of them. We may end up with five or six years of therapy with various people — having gotten only bits and pieces of insight to help us. The ego then has a tendency to blame all therapists as being no good. After all, haven't I tried enough of them to know? Chances are, if you have seen three or four, or more therapists for only a few weeks or months each and have not found one among them who could help you, the problem is not the therapists — at least not all of them. It is more probable that your ego's defense system has not allowed you to stay with one therapist long enough to get to your real problems.

Another part of the difficulty may be that for you, the place to start is not to work on your emotional problems, but to go directly to the real cause underlying the emotional and physical effects. That cause is always a lack of conscious contact with a Higher Power you are willing to believe in.

Of course, not all therapists are effective; not all therapists can work with all clients, and not all therapists are ethical. Also, in the past few years, a lot of pressure has arisen from clients and insurance companies for shorter and less expensive therapy. In part this has been in response to the long years required by psychoanalysis, which used to be the only well-known form of therapy as late as the fifties and even early sixties. But the pendulum may have swung too far the other way. In an effort to increase the number of clients and help more people more quickly, some therapists are advocating brief therapy which may be as short as eight or ten sessions. There is little doubt that this type of therapy is effective for people with minor or surface problems, but it is extremely doubtful that it can be helpful for removing the unconscious ego blocks which prevent the spiritual transformation we are exploring here.

One of the prime goals of therapy is for clients to learn to be their own therapists so they won't have to continue to see a therapist any longer than necessary. Those of us who have particularly stubborn or resistant egos will need to go to deeper levels to uncover the source of our problems and learn to accept all the unconscious material which our ego may have kept repressed for much of our lives. This takes time, and we need to give ourselves the necessary time if we want to accomplish anything of lasting value.

All of this makes the choice of therapist seem very complicated. How can we be sure we have the right one for us? Unfortunately, there are no guarantees that we will "hit it right" the first time. In spite of all the state examinations and licensing procedures, some "bad apples" do sneak through. Hopefully, most of these eventually weed themselves out, but a few seem to persist tenaciously and act in ways that may be harmful to clients.

It is beyond the scope of this book to go into detail about how to choose the right therapist for you, but a few general guidelines which you may find helpful are included in the Appendix.

Many of us have gone through various amounts and types of therapy in our search for the Higher Power within us. At the time, we didn't know that we were searching for a Higher Power we could believe in. We often made our therapist our Higher Power as we had many times before with so many of the "authorities" in our lives — parents, teachers, coaches, older relatives, friends, spouses, local or world "heroes," etc. Our egos are quick to grab onto any "Higher Power" they think can provide a solution. But our egos also like to acquire a Higher Power so they can blame it when things don't turn out the way the ego wants. "If it weren't for my parents, or my therapist, or my wife or husband, I could get what I (my ego) want(s)." Our ego doesn't allow us to realize that we cannot improve if we don't assume the responsibility for our own improvement. Blaming or finding fault with someone does exactly the opposite. It puts the responsibility on that someone to do the changing, or to change us, so we can feel better. That would be nice but it doesn't work. If that someone does change, he or they might begin to feel better, but we won't because no other person can make us feel better, except for very short intervals.

It is true that if someone has been hitting us on the head with a hammer and he stops, we feel better, but why do we insist on putting ourselves in the position where that person can do that? Why do we have to wait for him or her to stop? Why don't we just step aside and let the hammer fall on the chair or the floor instead of our head? *We* need to take the action — the first step out of the misery. If we wait for someone else to do it, we may wait forever.

Sometimes we are so far down in the depths of despair or depression that we cannot take the first step alone. Our egos are so much in control that we have become immobilized. It is impossible for us to move, even though we want to and try to. It is often at such times that we find the help we need — if we are willing. It may be going to a therapist — and that is taking a big first step — or calling a self/mutual help growth group such as

Emotional Health Anonymous or Overeaters Anonymous or Alcoholics Anonymous,* depending on what our Number One problem is.

These anonymous programs are also called Twelve Step Fellowships because they all use the same Twelve Steps to recovery developed so successfully by Alcoholics Anonymous. These steps are based on universal spiritual principles, and contain the wisdom of the ages. For many people, weekly or daily attendance at meetings of these groups are just what is needed to begin the journey to a spiritual awakening — that is the process of letting the "I"-part of us penetrate our ego-limited consciousness so it can begin its work of transforming us from ego-dominated "slaves" to God-guided, sincere, joyous, responsible persons aware of our oneness with God and all our fellow-parts of God.

Perhaps for you, the help you need will come through a religious group or social program. Remember that whatever path you take, make sure it has a heart at its core rather than only a mind, a philosophy or an ideology. There is no purer form of heart or love than God, but the path you choose must allow you to come to your own concept of God, rather than present you

*You can probably find O.A. or A.A. in your local phone directory. The EHA General Service Office address is: 2420 San Gabriel Blvd., Rosemead, CA 91770. The telephone numbers are: (818) 573-5482 or (213) 283-3574.

with someone else's interpretation. Your path must lead you gently deeper and deeper into yourself, give you the tools to help you recognize your ego and all its devious ways, and eventually, at your own pace, to penetrate past all your ego defenses to the very depths of your Soul where the only God there is resides.

Be aware that any path that insists or demands that you accept any dogma or "party line," no matter how enticing it sounds, or any path that places any restrictions on who may join or not join, probably does not have a heart at its core. Remember also that if the "Word of God" is interpreted by a leader or guru no matter how wise, and the path insists that you accept only that interpretation and no other, that restriction is an ego restriction and God's intentions have very likely been distorted in the translation. This is true because, by the very nature of God, He places no restrictions on us as to how to reach Him. He accepts us all equally and knows that our path to Him must be one of increasing freedom and learning to take responsibility for our own progress rather than depend on restrictions or interpretations imposed on us by other ego-bound individuals like ourselves. To provide guidance is one thing; to impose restrictive interpretations is quite another. If your path does not give you the freedom to accept or reject suggestions or guidance, to proceed in your own way and pace, to use only what is helpful to you at the moment and to forget the rest, then perhaps you need to ask yourself if you have chosen a path with a heart which will help you to find God in your own way within your own expanding consciousness.

Chapter 7
Surrender of the Ego

We have already seen how difficult it is for the ego to surrender. Our ego is so well defended that it will not allow anything to touch it. As soon as some of the defenses are cracked or damaged, it builds new ones to take their place. We have already touched on the defenses of denial and projection. Some others are self-deception, self-pity, illusion, rationalization, regression, image making and protecting, blaming, arguing, and worshiping. We all use these almost all the time in varying degrees. They are designed and applied unconsciously by the ego to further its mistaken belief that it must maintain control at all costs. During the whole time that our ego is applying these defenses, it is denying that it is doing so, and insisting that it is being honest. It will even argue vociferously that it doesn't understand what these defenses are, what they mean, or how it can do anything about them if all this is going on unconsciously. It will then become angry with this explanation of its behavior and refuse to look at it.

For as long as possible, the ego continues to insist that our problems are minor. If we just make this next external change, or go to this seminar, or take that course, everything will be all right. The external changes can also be job-related, geographic, more money, marital or relationship status, or anything else the ego can pin its hopes on for a solution or an improvement. Many of us who have tried these various forms of denial and escape know that they can provide temporary relief, but that the same or worse symptoms always return after the initial effect of the interim "solution" has worn off. We learn, sometimes through great pain, that nothing external can replace facing our inner selves and doing the work we need to do to learn to know and love ourselves.

Self-deception, which we all practice to varying degrees, is the ego telling us that we are something we're not. At one time in my life, I saw myself as a potential manager of great enterprises — an executive making important, far-reaching decisions and controlling large sums of money. My ego needed this image to convince itself that it (and I) was worthwhile — that I really was somebody important. This self-deception was necessary to keep my unconscious fear that I was a "nobody" from surfacing to consciousness. Since at the time, I was aware only of my ego and didn't know anything about my real "I" and my Higher Power, my ego rightly knew but did not want to face that it really is nobody, nothing, and does not even exist, except in its own imagination. To maintain control of me and my life, my ego had to maintain the deception that, if not now, at least some day, I would be a great executive. This is only one of the many self-deceptions the ego uses to preserve itself at our expense. I'm sure that as you become more honest with yourself, you will find at least half a dozen in your life. I know I found, and am still finding, more than that in mine. My ego continually used to tell me I was a great lover, a great father, a wonderful son, a really open and honest person, a model husband, a brilliant engineer, a top-notch manager, an independent person, and so on and on!

But the ego is never really sure that those great things it makes up about us are true. It would like to be sure and tries very hard to have us believe that these things are true, but no matter how many times the ego repeats these things to us and no matter how sure it sounds, there is always a part of itself that doubts. No matter how much evidence we get from the outside world, the ego is still doubtful. This is because the ego is split. As we have seen, one part of it is conscious and one part unconscious, and the two are usually at war with each other. If the conscious part of the ego is telling us how great we are and how we can do anything we set our mind to do, the unconscious part sets about trying to prove it isn't true through doubt, deception, confusion, and even sabotage. As we have seen, the unconscious part of the ego sometimes lets the conscious part control all the way until the final goal is almost in sight, and then steps in and causes us to blunder at the last minute to spoil it for ourselves.

When my ego wanted so badly for me to be a manager to prove to the world and to itself that it was somebody important, the harder I tried, the more the goal seemed to elude me. I always tried to sound very sure of myself — especially when I wasn't — as if I knew the answer to every problem. Quite often, when I opened my mouth, I would start to stutter, blunder, and mumble, sounding horribly unsure. Even though the answers were often right, my unconscious ego would not let me present them in a way that would convince my bosses that I knew what I was doing.

But everything which appears to be a failure has a positive side which we can use to further our growth. If we realize that our ego, when operating on its own, is always bound to fail, then we can look beyond these "failures" to see what lesson our "I" is trying to learn from it. In this case, the lesson for me to learn was not to become too attached to my ego's goals because that attachment blocks the inner guidance from my Higher Power. When I am so bent on pursuing my ego's goals, I am not interested in and cannot hear the Inner Guidance. My ego is in charge and filters out everything that is not in line with its will. Even when my ego temporarily succeeds in achieving what it wants, it will almost always fail in the long run.

When our ego's will is in line with our Higher Power's will for us (which only occurs when our ego has surrendered), there is no problem. There is only harmony and smooth flow in our lives. All the doors open at exactly the right time and we are given all the abilities and materials we need to carry out God's will for us which is also our true will. But when the ego decides to go off on its own, as all egos do until they learn better, obstacles arise everywhere. And *they always come from within ourselves, even when they appear to be originating outside.* We find ourselves unable to do what our ego tells us we should do easily, and nothing goes smoothly. It all becomes an uphill battle and we usually end up full of resentments, blaming everyone around us and the world as well.

When I was so eager to become a manager for all the wrong (ego) reasons, promotions continually eluded me. I was passed over for other men who were more ready, but I couldn't accept that. Each time, I felt more inadequate; and unwilling to show it or admit it, I would redouble my efforts and try again. After all, isn't it true that, "If at first you don't succeed, try, try again?" and again and again?

I reached a point after several years of trying harder where I didn't have any trying left in me. I (my ego) decided that if they didn't want me as a manager, I would go and get my significance and prestige elsewhere. I stopped trying for a promotion and instead, went back to school to work on a Ph.D. degree. A few weeks after I started the preparatory courses, I was promoted at work to Project Manager, a few months later to Branch Manager, and two years after that to Department Manager, reporting to a corporate vice-president.

How do I explain that? One explanation seems to be that when the ego becomes willing to let go of something it wants obsessively and which it is unable to attain, then, that very thing happens. As long as the conscious ego is trying desperately to achieve that goal, the unconscious part of the ego sets up a greater inner resistance which prevents it from coming about. It's as if all our energy is bound up in this internal ego struggle, and therefore not available to use toward accomplishing the goal. This seems especially true if the ego's motive is to make us more apparently secure or more important in this material world that the ego lives in.

Another explanation is that when we (our conscious ego) let(s) go, the inner unconscious resistance disappears also. The inner ego war stops. Then our Higher Power is able to give us that which we wanted. His energy can flow through us unobstructed by our inner struggles, and can therefore manifest as positive experience in our lives. Because we are often unaware of both our inner unconscious resistance and the Higher Power within us, we don't understand why we're so often denied what we want. We actually deny it to ourselves by wanting it too much and wanting it for ego reasons: e.g., supposed self-worth, a false sense of importance, wanting power over others, wanting a "secure" place in the world, or "taking care of Number 1." The self-destructiveness of our ego thus shuts off the good which only our Higher Power can give us.

Another way of saying this is that all of us really have to learn about the goodness, generosity, and abundance of God — our Higher Power — all of which is within us. We cannot learn this lesson if our conscious ego continually calls the shots. Since the ego is insane, it always works against itself to deny itself what it wants.

The lesson we need to learn is that our Higher Power is always ready to give us everything the moment the ego surrenders. But for most of us, the ego, being well-entrenched within us from years of reinforcement by ourselves and the culture we live in, does not surrender easily. At certain times, during rare moments of openness, we may experience brief periods of direct contact with God. These experiences always have a mystical or miraculous aura to them. When they end, we return to ego-oriented functioning, although perhaps a step closer to the Great Power within. These temporary occurrences of surrender can create great frustration in our lives. This happens when our ego tries to take control of the experience and begins to insist that we must live our lives in such contact with God on a permanent basis. By this attempt at control to *make* the experience happen again and last longer, the ego sets up exactly the kind of conflict we have just mentioned. It sets itself up to destroy what it wants most. The ego doesn't want to hear that the only way to reach God is through its own surrender. It wants to take charge of the process and make it happen *now*! For most of us, the process of ego surrender is a gradual one which takes place by little tiny steps — each one of which is barely visible. Any attempt by the ego to rush it or find shortcuts slows it down. Perhaps that is as it is meant to be. Since God is "invisible," we proceed toward this Loving Infinity with steps so small that each one in itself is invisible.

According to the Bible, Moses spent forty days and forty nights on Mount Sinai before he came down with the Ten Commandments given him by God . . . and Jesus spent forty days and forty nights in the desert being tested by temptation after temptation from his ego. Although these were relatively brief periods, they were preceded by years of gradual preparation without which the forty days would probably have produced no result. The Buddha, another truly spiritual being, spent six years or more searching for enlightenment before spending one entire night under the Bodhi Tree which culminated in his awakening. Subsequent to this momentous event, he spent 49 more days getting acclimated to his new state of higher consciousness before his transformation was complete. Since most of us are surely not as advanced as Moses, Buddha, or Jesus, it might not be too surprising if our transformation process which is a gradual surrender of the ego, takes a bit longer.

I started my transformation process 29 years ago, before I even knew that that's what I was doing. Because I was so turned off to anything spiritual in my youth, as a part of my rebellion against semi-religious parents, I had to begin through psychotherapy. My ego was so overblown and arrogant at the time that I couldn't even admit that I needed the therapy. At age 21, I married a young woman who had neurotic problems which to me, seemed much greater than my own. I was going to "save" her and make her well. I proceeded to concentrate on her problems in order to "help" her, but really to hide my own. She developed migraine headaches, breathing difficulties, uncontrollable fears, and depression. For three years, we tried to have a baby, but couldn't. After exhausting all the physiological medicine avenues, we thought that psychotherapy might help. At that point, she said wisely, "I won't go unless you go too." So I went — not because I needed it, mind you — but because that was the only way I could get her to go. Or so my ego said. Actually, I needed it as much as she, and through six years of therapy with a very good psychiatrist, I learned the extent to which I really did need it.

I learned that I was an unfeeling, inconsiderate, self-centered, frightened, rigid, dependent person who had great expectations and grandiose ideas about what he was to do on this earth, and was emotionally completely incapable of carrying them out. I just couldn't be president or even vice-president of my company by the time I was 30. Carefully evaluating my progress in ego-time, I thought it wholly inadequate of myself to be as old as 39 by the time I was promoted to Department Manager. My whole life and worth were centered on my career. I neither realized nor acknowledged the extent to which my wife and two children and our home in the hills overlooking the San Fernando Valley of Los Angeles provided the anchor and security I needed to function at all.

At the end of six years of therapy in 1963, my ego was stronger than ever. I redoubled my efforts at obtaining a promotion at work. Since I was now emotionally "certified," there could be no reason (as far as my ego could see) why I should not become a manager. I spent the next three years trying to convince my boss that I was "executive material." As I related earlier, when that didn't happen, I gave up and went back to school to obtain a Ph.D. degree in management. If my ego couldn't manipulate itself into prestige and status in one way, it would find another.

As I mentioned, as soon as I enrolled at school, the promotions came at work. I was amazed. I couldn't believe that when I wanted something very badly, I couldn't get it, but when I let go of it, there it was — practically dumped in my lap. My ego, being as strong as it was, tried to convince me that I could do both: go to school, work on a Ph.D. and at the same time, handle heavy management responsibilities. After burning the candle at both ends for two years, I ended up so physically sick that during a period of three months, I couldn't get out of bed for more than two days at a time. After that, I got up, went to work for a few days, resuming my frantic pace, and ended up in bed again for a week. That's the insanity of the ego again. Through the pain and sickness, my ego finally began to realize that it had to surrender a bit. I would have to choose: management now or Ph.D. now, but not both. I chose management and dropped out of school.

Within a year, I was a Department Manager as I had wanted to be for so long, and the following two years were the most miserable of my life. These were the rewards of achieving an ego goal. I lived in constant fear of being fired or replaced. At times, the fear was so strong that it was paralyzing. I knew exactly what to do to impress my bosses and keep my job, yet was often totally incapable of putting it into action. I would shake when giving management briefings and thought everyone could see it. I found myself going to sleep in top management meetings with customers when I should have been alert and wide awake, and glued to my chair when I should have been on my feet speaking my piece. I became increasingly silent, sullen, withdrawn and hostile — utterly frightened and demoralized. Yet my ego was saying, "Pull yourself together; you can make it; don't let them see what's going on inside you, and you'll be OK."

About the time I made the decision to drop out of school, I was led — again through the doings of my wife (although she didn't know it) — to a fellowship for emotional and spiritual growth. I went to meetings — again, supposedly to help my wife, rather than because I needed it (according to my ego). She had an incurable disease and the people in this fellowship knew how to understand and live with people who have this disease. I went also because my psychiatrist suggested it when I told him about the problem, and because I wanted to learn what these people knew about this disease. All good ego reasons. In reality I went to those meetings because the "I" within me — whom I didn't recognize or acknowledge at the time — knew that my ego needed to learn some spiritual lessons in a way which would be palatable to it, and guided me there as gently as my ego would allow.

At that point, my ego had already surrendered enough to make it possible for me to sit through one meeting each week and take in at least some of what was said. My ego didn't agree with much of what it heard and didn't understand a great deal of it. But I kept coming back. Unconsciously, I sensed there was an answer there for me for which I had been searching a long time.

The path to surrender is different for each of us. Because our egos have been crazy for so long, it usually involves some pain. For those with the tougher egos, the pain can be excruciating and can last a long time. Hopefully, this will not be so for you. The one thing which is true for all of us is that we can't seem to predict the point when we will be ready to surrender, and we can't chart the course. It is something each of us comes to in his/her own time and way, and it takes what it takes. It may help us to remember that what causes our pain is not growth or surrender, it is our ego's resistance to these, and our great fear that our ego's surrender will be followed by nothingness for us. In fact, it is the doorway to Everythingness.

Chapter 8
Growing Awareness of a Higher Power

At some point in our lives, we become aware that there is a Power greater than ourselves at work somewhere. So many strange things have been said and written about God that many of us are exposed to Him in a negative way during our childhood. Since these childhood patterns are deeply ingrained in our unconscious ego mind, we often don't realize how many negative ideas we carry around with us and what a heavy burden these hidden ideas are.

Some of us don't trust God because He lets all those terrible things happen in the world. We feel He shouldn't let "innocent" people be hurt or killed. He shouldn't allow wars to happen. Somehow, He should make sure everyone is always nice, kind, and loving to everyone else. We don't realize how contradictory these beliefs are and therefore how untrue they are. We usually defend our false beliefs and our right to believe falseness rather than truth with all the strength and anger our egos can muster. Some people even get angry when we say that God created us or even just that God IS. Some people get turned off by the word God. I was one of those people. If you said anything to me about God, I got inwardly angry and tuned you out. If I could, I got rid of you as fast as I could and had as little contact with you as possible.

Those negative ideas about God are contradictory because in one breath we say that God created us and gave us free will, the will to be anything we desire, and in the next breath we say we want God to control "bad" people and make them "good." The point is that God is perfectly consistent, not contradictory. When He gives us freedom, He gives us unconditional freedom — no strings attached. He does not give us freedom only if we're "good" and imprisonment or punishment if we're "bad." Only egos do that, not God. God's guidance is always clear, consistent, and true. God does not know how to tell a lie. He merely creates with love and truth, and endows with all His Love everything He creates. In fact, He places Himself and His Love which are inseparable, at the very core of everything He creates, including every one of us.

We are the ones who, when under control of our egos, forget that at one time we knew we were all part of God because God is all there is. There can be nothing real outside God. Though we have forgotten it, all of us are still part of God today because He is still all there is today. God never changes. He is Infinite Love and Perfection yesterday, today, and forever. And we are also because He made each one of us out of Himself in His own Image and Likeness.

We are the ones, under control of our egos, who forget that we are a part of Him. We shut

Him off and stop listening to His loving Guidance. We are the ones who wander away and create an ego which sees bad and good. We allow our egos to separate us into good, better, best, and worse. We are the ones who, having turned away from Him, put our egos in His place and fall into doubt and suspicion. We lose faith and trust. We become physically and mentally ill. We learn to control, manipulate, compete, judge, criticize, and eventually hate those who are different from us. We forget God to the extent that we become our egos. We invent words like spick, dago, kike, goon, nigger, and wasp to separate ourselves from those we fear or hate because we see them to be not as good as we, or better than we. We are the ones who cheat, steal, kill, murder each other. We are the ones who go to war because we see our nation as being better than another or because we fear that another nation will attack us or take something that belongs to us.

We are the ones who make all these separations and distinctions, not God. God still sees us only as part of His Infinite Goodness and Perfection because He knows that He is at the very center of every one of us and that sooner or later, we will awaken spiritually and come back to this great Center from which we have apparently strayed.

Some of us believe that God punishes us for all these "bad" things. We tend to think of Him as a stern parent who must discipline His children because that is what our parents did with us. But again, this cannot be because it is not consistent with the Infinite Love God is and gives us. Loving unconditionally as He does, God does not love us only when we're "good" and punishes us when we're "bad." Good and bad are qualities egos invented. They are not known to God because God is all One, not two; all good, not good and bad. He merely waits for us to be finished with our individual antics of separateness, greed, fear and the mayhem that results from these. He knows full well that when we're finished learning that separation, hate and pride will not work, we will come back to his Love. *There's nowhere else to go.* He knows full well that when we used our free will to separate from Him as He had *not* intended, our ego grew to fill the gap created by the separation, and that this ego has now hoodwinked us into believing that it and all the world it has made are real; and that God is unreal.

God knows all this and is willing to accept us just as we are and to forgive all the "bad" things we think we may have done. Since in His "eyes" there are no "bad" things, He knows that His forgiveness is not needed for Him. But because in our eyes, there are many bad things, we need to forgive ourselves and each other; and to know that He forgives us — at least until we reach the point where we come to know that there are no sins to be forgiven, only ego errors to let go of.

So we see that great numbers of us have so many false ideas about God and because they are false, we get confused and decide to have nothing to do with Him at all. Our ego thus grows bigger and stronger, and builds greater defenses to resist any new idea of God that might be presented to us. Since to the ego, the best defense is a strong offense, it attacks vigorously any idea about God that might be different from its own current beliefs, whether these beliefs are true or false.

Some of us who have gone through a great deal of pain from mental anguish to physical ailments know that these result only from an ego gone beserk. We also know that there is good in this crazy path the ego takes because it is the only way our ego will reach that point of surrender where it will let itself become aware that a Power greater than itself may exist, and that it might ease things a bit to learn to listen to that Power.

Many of us become willing to find this Power within ourselves only after many hospitalizations in mental institutions, numerous heart attacks, several surgeries of various kinds, suicide attempts or repeated bouts with diseases of all kinds. Some of our egos are so strong and so set in their ways that nothing will penetrate their defenses other than extreme physical and mental pain and complete lack of self-esteem. The part that seems so strange to many of us is that these extremely low "bottoms" often don't occur until two to six years after the start of our ego's surrender process. It seems as though after that time, the ego puts up a last ditch stand to attempt to regain lost control or to keep from losing more control. Whether it is successful or not depends *not* on our trying harder to keep our ego from doing that, but more on how willing we are to learn a new way of life based on letting go and letting God help us by allowing our "I" to transform us into new God-centered beings.

Many of us don't have to go to these low extremes. Perhaps our ego surrenders with somewhat less resistance. For any number of reasons, we allow the Higher Power within us to reach our conscious awareness sooner. But to some degree, the ego must reach a point where it realizes, "I can't do it alone," or "I can't stand it any more," or "I need help; please help me." This is always a call to God, although we may not recognize it at the time; and it is often answered by a single human being. There is a story about that which many of you may have heard but I'll repeat it for those who haven't. Joe and Tom were standing next to each other at a bar. Joe said: "I don't believe in God; He's never done anything for me." Tom asked "How come? That sounds strange." Joe told him that the previous year, he had been on an expedition in the Arctic region and a big storm came up. He said: "I got lost, separated from the group, wandered about for days — no food, no heat. I thought I was going to die." Tom remarked, "But you're here; what happened? Didn't God save you?" "No," said Joe, "God didn't have anything to do with it. Some Eskimo just happened to come along and find me!"

Nothing that "saves" us just happens to come along. There are no coincidences — only miracles. God is at work all the time just waiting for us to become ready to accept His generous help. The process of my becoming ready occurred through the growth fellowship meetings I spoke of earlier. Very slowly and gradually, my ego resistance was overcome and I began to practice some of the things the people in the meetings were saying had helped them.

They said, "If anything in your life is causing you too much trouble or pain, turn it over to your Higher Power. Let go of it; don't try to solve it yourself; ask Him or It to guide you to the answer. Then become willing to go along with that answer." They also said, "Keep coming back" a lot! They told me it didn't matter what kind of Higher Power I believed in so long as it was greater than myself. They suggested I begin to look at all the nice coincidences in my life as miracles — especially the small ones — and to thank my Higher Power for every one of them. They said that feeling gratitude is one of the most spiritual and healing attitudes which eventually leads us to learn how to love. What is a small miracle? When the rain stops just at the time I'm ready to go outside; when the light turns green just as I approach it; when you get a raise or an unexpected check in the mail; when you find a space in a crowded parking lot; when the cold you thought you were catching doesn't materialize; when a stranger smiles at you in the market. The list is endless. I know if you just try a little, you can add many more of your own.

Of course, if you're like I was, you ask, "What do I do when the light turns red as I approach it?" People in the fellowship said, "You call that a miracle too, and thank your Higher Power for a chance to pause and say thank You." I found it especially helpful to pause when I'm in a hurry, because that's often when the lights turn red. It's quite possible that pausing for a light saved me from hurrying to an accident.

It's interesting how many miracles you find in your life when you begin to put this simple little bit of guidance into practice. The more you do it, the more often the lights begin to turn green, and parking spaces open up, and you find the last item on the market shelf you thought was empty. God does help those who help themselves, and we help ourselves by being grateful for "little" things and by being good to ourselves.

The people in those meetings also said, "stop judging, criticizing, blaming and complaining." That's a toughie! Very hard to put in practice for a tough ego like mine. Blaming and criticizing is the ego's stock in trade. That's what it likes to do best to everyone — ourselves included. Getting my ego to stop doing those things which only harm me has been one of the hardest things I've had to do. I can only do it by letting my Higher Power do it and cooperating with Him to the best of my ability. But it has taught me patience, and also that my ego won't be pushed or rushed. I've learned that my ego responds to gentleness. It can be taught; it can learn and it can change; but it insists on doing it at its own pace. If I (my conscious ego) tries to rush or push, my unconscious ego fights back more and slows me down. It is no different in this process of growth than it is for the ego's own goals. When I'm rushing, pushing, and impatient, it's my ego that has gotten hold of the new goal and is doing the pushing. The ego wants instant results. It says, "OK, you want to improve? You want to be spiritual? You want to accept God's guidance? Then hurry up about it! What's the matter with you, you slow poke? Can't you learn anything? You *should* be further along by now. Why don't you practice what you preach? Put your money where your mouth is, and walk like you talk — perfectly — all the time!"

We have seen that the more the ego does this pushing, the more resistance it puts up internally to accomplishing the goal it clamors for externally. The Higher Power never pushes

143

because He has infinite patience. He knows that we are all on our way to remembering we're all part of Him because there's nowhere else to go. He realizes that some of us may take long detours in the paths we choose toward this goal because we need to learn these lessons in our own way and could not learn them any other way.

Our Higher Power knows that if we could find an easier, softer way, we would. He knows that our ego is cunning, baffling, and powerful, and that it doesn't surrender easily. And He also knows that sooner or later *every* ego will surrender, will collapse because the ego is not real. It is merely the idol we have made up to take the place of God in the gap we created when we chose to disregard Him and go our own external way. So there is hope for every one of us even though at times our egos make things so black that we are tricked into believing there is no hope.

I continued to practice these little things people in the fellowship shared with me until they became easier and easier to do. As I did this, "little" miracle followed "little" miracle until I began to see, very dimly at first, that *whether an event or situation is a miracle or not depends much more on my attitude about it than on the event or situation itself.* I also began to see that there are no *big* or *little* miracles; there are only miracles. A miracle is anything God does which the ego cannot understand. And God does more and more for us as we learn how to let Him. The ego is the part of us that calls some miracles big and some little — not God. Those are ego judgments because God doesn't judge. He just IS.

On this spiritual road, there are lessons to be learned in *everything,* and we begin to learn these lessons when we can stop judging people, places, and things as good or bad, right or wrong, desirable or undesirable. When we remove the judgment labels, then we can see the person or place or event as it truly is, rather than our ego's judgment of it which is always distorted. From this new undistorted view, we learn the lessons we're supposed to learn. We need only do our "footwork," part of which is to stop blaming, judging, and complaining; let go of the results; and our Higher Power does the rest.

Chapter 9
The Emerging of the "I"

It is difficult to believe the things we have been saying without trying them and experiencing them yourself. You can read what I'm writing and be either turned off or turned on by it. None of it will help you in your life until you begin to put it in practice yourself. It may not even work very well if you try it grudgingly or skeptically, but even then, it will work to a degree. To give yourself the best chance, you need to recognize that you *have* an ego, but that you *are not* your ego. You need to see at least to some degree that your ego has gotten you into a lot of trouble, or has stood in the way of getting what you really want. Even if your ego has gotten you what you thought you wanted, you find at some point that those things are what your ego wanted — not you. The sure way to experience this is when you want something for a long time and you really work for it, and finally you get it. Then you suddenly find you don't get the satisfaction from it you thought you would. Or, you enjoy it for a while, but the enjoyment fades away quickly. That happens because the thing you wanted and got was your ego's goal rather than your "I" 's. It doesn't matter if it's a material object such as a car or a house, or something more intangible such as a college degree. These are all ego goals and they produce the same short-lived satisfaction.

If you are tired of pursuing one ego goal after another, all of which sooner or later turn to ashes in your mouth, you must really *want* to shed the life of the ego — at least to some extent. You must really *want* to find a better way, even if you don't know what that is yet. Then you need to become aware and eventually come to believe that there is a Power greater than your ego in the Universe, even if you don't know what that Power is or where to look for it. It is not important to know what this Power is or to understand it or grasp it, or even accept that it is within you at this point. It is important only that you accept the possibility of the existence of such a Power. This Power need not be God for you. You may think of It as expressing Itself through the members of the growth group you attend — especially if your group is a Twelve Step group like Alcoholics Anonymous, Emotional Health Anonymous, or Overeaters Anonymous. Members of these groups share their Higher Power with each other at meetings without even knowing that they're doing it. If you go to one of these meetings regularly, you can't help but become aware of a Power greater than yourself. It will rub off on you in spite of your ego — unless your ego is still extremely powerful.

Whether you have been a religious person all your life or rejected religion very early in life, or never had a religious upbringing doesn't matter at all. The Twelve Step groups are not religious but they do help you become aware of a Spiritual Force within the Universe. Eventually, when you're ready, you find this Spiritual Energy within you, and you may wish to call it God, as many people do. But even that is not necessary for spiritual growth. It just seems to become automatic after a while, because God is such a neat, short word and so easy to say. Chances are when that happens for you, your concept of God will be vastly different than the one you started with. Most of us start with an ego concept of God.

At the beginning, when we think we're all ego, we don't know the difference between "I" and ego. Our ego thinks that if there is a God, He must be just like the ego, so it imbues God (its own idea of Him) with all its own attributes and faults. The ego thinks of God as capable of being angry, impatient, whimsical, demanding, judging, punishing, because those are all the things the ego is. The ego thinks God is to be worshiped, feared, appeased, and often manipulated into running the world according to the ego's way. It is inconceivable to the ego that God could be not only the exact opposite of all these negative characteristics, but the exact opposite to an infinite degree!

When we begin to realize the true nature of God even to a very slight degree, our lives immediately begin to change. We begin to have hope that we need not continue to suffer as we have, that life can be fun, joyous, beautiful because that is the way God is, and God is within each of us. We begin the long, slow process of learning how to live such a life.

At this point, we begin to be more clearly aware of the two apparent forces within us, our ego which is not real because it is not of God, and our Higher Power which is the only Reality and Truth there is. When we become more willing to forego the ways of the ego and attempt to espouse those of the Higher Power, or to learn to receive the grace of God, our "I" is finally able to perform its transformation task. Though this process usually takes place out of our awareness, our "I" slowly appears to separate from our ego and to become the individual entity centered on and in God that it has always been. We begin to see that "I" have a choice. We often experience conflicts between our ego's way of doing things and our Higher Power's guidance. At first, we're distressed by so many conflicts, not being sure which way to go. We realize more and more that the ego's ways bring pain but we're afraid to let go of these old ideas because we don't yet trust our Higher Power enough.

As we become better observers of our own psychic processes, we realize more and more that we're choosing to try our Higher Power's way rather than the old ego ways. If someone insults us, we respond by asking God to bless that person and ourselves, praying for him or her rather than hurling back a similar insult. At first, we may do these things only because someone has told us that they work. As we learn more, and allow our Higher Power to teach us through our "I," we realize that every human being is a part of God. That includes us and everybody else. So if another person insults us, it is that person's ego that is trying to insult our ego — because that is the only part of us that can be insulted. The God part of us cannot be insulted because He doesn't recognize insult; only ego does. As our "I" observes this, "I" can see both the ego part and the Higher Power part of each of us, and "I" know that if I let ego take over, ego will respond with an equal or worse insult. But if ego surrenders to the point where I can operate freely, I will always choose my Higher Power's way, which is to bless the other person who is also a part of God. I will also pray that her/his ego will surrender to the point where it will stop trying to insult another part of God who cannot be insulted.

"I" realizes that ego always insults and attacks because ego is always full of fear and those are the means — insult and attack — it uses to protect itself. I also realize that my ego unconsciously attacks itself, because underneath all the disguises, deceptions and bravado, ego feels horribly unworthy, unlovable, and unacceptable. But not wanting to accept this self-attack, it hurls its own negative characteristics onto another person. In this way, ego can stay pure and innocent in its own eyes, keeping only "good" qualities for itself and avoiding dealing with anything which might mar its image. Thus the ego creates the world of good and bad, me versus them, me-good versus them-bad.

When ego begins to surrender, it gradually becomes willing to stop playing deceptive games. This can be painful at times because all the "bad" the ego thinks it has done rises up from its unconscious dungeons where it has been kept prisoner for years, and demands to be accepted. We slowly learn to face these imagined "sins" and to turn them over to our "I" for transformation into positive and constructive qualities and actions. "I" then begins to accept and forgive the "unforgivable" and we feel as though a very heavy weight has been lifted from our shoulders. I learn that I have committed no crimes or sins that cannot be forgiven, though my ego has made many mistakes that I need to correct. I begin to correct these mistakes when my ego surrenders and becomes willing to let my Higher Power's will for me be done. This will is the same as the will of my "I," my true will, and it is opposite to my ego's apparent will.

At this point, I become able to turn my ego's will and my life over to the care of the Higher Power within me, however I may conceive of such a Power. As I learn to do this in more of my life's situations, I grow in consciousness and awareness of myself as a true spirit. I grow in faith and in trust. I see myself more as I truly am — very close to my Higher Power — and it becomes more and more clear that the greater my ego's surrender, the happier, more creative, and more prosperous my life becomes. All of these — happiness, creativity, productivity, and prosperity — come to us as a result of our ego's surrender. They are not things we can or must work for by the sweat of our brow in pain and sorrow. They are gifts of God which are given to us in proportion to the degree of our ego's surrender and our letting our "I" transform us into the children of God we already are.

Chapter 10
Looking Into Ourselves

This path of spiritual growth we are describing seems arduous indeed, perhaps even impossible. At times, we wish we had never started. The pain of spiritual birth or rebirth seems greater than the rewards. At such times we need to remember how cunning our ego is and how many devious barriers it constantly raises in our path. We need also to realize at a very deep level that no matter how strong our ego seems to be, the Higher Power within us is infinitely stronger. In fact, when the dark recesses of the ego are finally exposed to the brilliant light of our Higher Power, the ego's imagined power begins to crumble, to disintegrate before our very eyes.

To expose the hidden recesses of our ego to the light of God is one of the most difficult processes we must go through. Many try to avoid doing it and desperately attempt to find shortcuts — easier, softer ways. Our ego is very helpful in this, since the last thing it wants is to be exposed. It does not want its tricks, deceptions, cover-ups, and ruses discovered for in these lie its imagined strength. As soon as seen for what they are, all these illusions become the paper tigers they truly are. But our ego will conspire with every other ego in the world to keep this from happening. To this end, all egos unconsciously conspire to make it as painful as possible for us to look into ourselves. They use the subterfuge of blaming, shame, guilt, negative thoughts, justifications, self-righteousness, self-pity, and extreme anger, among others, to make the process of looking into ourselves so painful that we will not look. If these tactics don't work, they resort to self-abasement and self-negation, often through physical or mental illness.

We may avoid looking for a time while our ego continues its delaying tactics, but sooner or later, the pain of not looking begins to outweigh the pain of looking. We continually repeat the same mistakes in our lives. We choose again and again the "wrong" people to be with. We "fail" constantly to achieve the goals our egos have set up and consequently feel increasingly worthless. We feel driven by forces within us we don't understand, and constantly look for an outside source to blame it on and to "fix" it. We increasingly try to control, manipulate and even beg the people close to us, not realizing how hopeless these attempts are, and how progressively more powerless we become. When we fail, we try harder and fail again — harder. Eventually, we give up in anger, disgust, and often depression, blaming the world around us and even God for our problems. Why doesn't He fix it for us?

At some point, we reach another place of surrender. We become sick and tired of being sick and tired. And we learn that the only way our egos will ever become tame is to give ourselves the time we need to look at the ego's subterfuges as they occur and have occurred in our lives. We remind ourselves once more that the God within us, the Spiritual Power, is what we truly are. As such, we cannot do anything morally wrong which must be punished or forgiven; but our egos have made many mistakes which we (I) need to correct.

The process usually works best when we write down our "inventories." This allows us to be more systematic. We know and remember which ego mistakes or defects we have found and to what depth we have gone with each. For many of us, writing temporarily turns off the conscious ego and establishes a direct connection with our unconscious. This is helpful because one of the deceptions the ego uses is that when we find a truth the ego doesn't want to face, it conveniently forgets, and thus doesn't have to do anything about it. It can continue its game of deceiving us and itself. Writing helps to neutralize that ego defense. Once committed to paper, the ego has a much harder time forgetting because the paper is always there for us to refer back to and to refresh its memory.

We search gently and patiently for all the resentments, fears, guilt, shame, pride, hate, lack of self-worth, and desire to control we have ever felt, and write them all down because these are the deceptions our ego uses to avoid facing the truth. We write down all the controlling, criticizing, condemning, judging, manipulating, people pleasing, pushing people away that we can recall having done, and realize that we need not punish or put ourselves down for these things any more. We have suffered enough already. We remember that we are a child of God who is within us, and that in His eyes, we can do no wrong. We can stray away from His grace, and then our egos grow and make all kinds of mistakes. But the ill effects of these mistakes are forgiven the instant the ego becomes willing to surrender. At that point, "I" transforms our mistakes into strengths and capabilities which will be of help to our fellow human beings.

Taking an inventory requires much patience of us. It is not something that can be dashed off in a matter of hours or even days. It may require several weeks or months, doing a little at a time. For most of us, it becomes an ongoing process. On a daily basis, we need to look at our ego to be aware of the new illusions and delusions it constantly cooks up. The surrender of the ego is a life-time job which we do a day at a time. For those who believe it, it is a process that may stretch over many life-times.

Some of us may tend to rush the process of looking into ourselves. Our egos seem to believe that if we can take the "crash course" and rush through it, it will all be behind us and we need never look again. As we have seen before, rushing the process is another way the ego hinders us. It resists doing it in depth while appearing to be gung-ho on the surface. Such apparent rushing by the conscious ego almost always sets up unconscious resistance which eventually slows the process. In this case, the resistance often takes the form of denial, "There's really nothing wrong; I had a beautiful childhood." Or "Looking at the past won't help; I want to find out what's wrong with me *now!*" It can also take the form of delay, "I'm not ready yet," or "Better not look further; I might lose my mind." We don't realize that as long as we're under control of the ego, we have already lost our minds and what we're trying to do is to find them again by clearing away the wreckage of past negative emotions, beliefs and attitudes.

Rushing our development or striving with all our (ego's) might to do it "right" is not what it's about. It is more a matter of relaxing, realizing that our ego needs time before it feels safe enough to surrender. What we can do is build patience enough to accept our ego's pace, resistance and sabotage. We need to develop the observer part of ourselves and tone down the judgmental so that we can find, a bit at a time, all e material within us that our ego has kept buried for years — so that we can find all this buried hurt, resentment, sorrow, guilt, pride, self-centeredness, and truly say: "These things are mine. Many, if not all of them, were errors I (my ego) committed because without realizing it, I allowed myself to become a slave of my ego." When we can accept all of this buried pain, shame and guilt without judging ourselves or others negatively, and realizing that we were doing the best we knew, then we can become increasingly honest and sincerely ask for our Higher Power's help in allowing "I" to transform us.

Another way the ego resists is by flipping to the opposite pole. Instead of, "There's nothing wrong, everything is fine," it flips to, "Everything is wrong; I'm the most terrible person on earth; I've done terrible, unforgivable things; no one loves me or ever will; I hate myself; this misery will never end; I'll just continue repeating those same horrible things forever; the only answer is to kill myself. That way, I'll end the pain, end the suffering, end everything." This is the ego in reverse, another of its many disguises. It is important for us to recognize those all too familiar phrases as a disguise of the ego; otherwise we might be tempted to believe all those lies and do away with ourselves. Aye, there's the rub. Some of us have believed for a long time that when we kill ourselves, we don't end everything. There is mounting evidence that we kill only our body and that a part of our ego, as well as our "I" which is our individual expression of the Universal Spirit, continues and lives forever. This individual part of the Universal Spirit with the non-physical ego constitutes our Soul which does not die. Being of Spirit, it is eternal.

If this is true, suicide doesn't solve the problem as we might hope. We take our unfinished ego business with us beyond the physical grave and must continue to try to resolve it there. Unless we're in acute physical pain, the reasons we think of committing suicide are usually not physical. They are mental and emotional. They are especially attitudinal. These are all things we need to change by learning and realizing our true nature as a perfect creation of God. If we don't complete our learning in this life, then we probably will continue the process in a future one. We cannot erase emotional and attitudinal problems by ending the life of the body. Since these errors in our attitudes are in our minds — more specifically the ego part of our minds, they don't end when the body dies. The evidence in the books of Ruth Montgomery, Edgar Cayce, Jane Roberts and others seem to indicate that we come to physical life to learn certain lessons from our experiences here. If we cut our time here short by committing suicide, chances are we will have to come back to continue our education where we left off. So we are likely to find ourselves right back at the same place we thought we left.

Except in rare instances, suicide — even when "successful" in the ego sense — is an attempted escape that backfires as escaping always does. There seems to be no way out of our predicament except to continue to move forward toward God — toward the Higher Power within us. The more we can gently teach our ego consciously to help our "I" in the process of transforming us to the point where we realize our unity with God, the faster the process will be. But we must remember to be gentle and not too eager about it.

The desire to die and thoughts of suicide may also result because at some point in our lives, when things looked very black to us, perhaps even as children, we consciously or unconsciously experienced the wish to be dead. Many of us grew up as unwanted children, emotionally abandoned by parents who didn't have the capacity to love us. Perhaps we were wanted at first, but when our parents realized the responsibility involved in raising a child, they couldn't live up to it and wished they hadn't had us. Our parents may have told us this in one or more moments of anger. Or we may have sensed the message even if our parents didn't allow themselves to know it consciously. Wanting to comply with our parents' unconscious wishes, we unconsciously decided that everyone would be better off if we were dead. They wouldn't have the burden of raising us, and we could avoid the pain of growing up unwanted and unloved.

Others of us have had a parent die when we were very young — perhaps even both parents — and grew up as orphans or with only one parent. Again our single parent or guardians may have felt that the burden of raising us was more than they were capable of. Although they did the best they could, our ego picked up the overtly or indirectly given message that we were a heavy burden. We may have unconsciously decided that we should die to relieve those we depended on, and perhaps loved, of this heavy load. If the parent who died was the one we preferred, the wish to die may have been compounded by an unconscious wish to join our dead, beloved parent. We might also have locked up inside us great feelings of guilt, feeling responsible for our parent's death and strong anger at him or her for having left us in the hands of a parent whom we felt didn't really care for us or about us.

For most of us, such feelings would be so unacceptable and so painful to experience as children that our egos protected us by keeping them out of our consciousness. But when we embark on a spiritual journey, knowingly or unknowingly, we also commit ourselves to self-honesty and self-discovery. As our ego surrenders, bit by bit, these unresolved, hidden feelings from our past begin to emerge. If we had strong unexpressed or not fully expressed desires to die, these will come up as well and may, at times, seem overwhelming unless we recognize them for what they are. Here a skillful therapist can help us to see how our current feelings have their origins in our past, and help us maintain a better perspective while we go through the experience of separating ourselves in the present from the little child and parents of our past.

If we realize that to continue our spiritual growth, we must allow the removal of any unconscious blocks caused by accumulated, unresolved emotional feelings or conflicts; and if we can honestly look at our past and, as we are able to, recall and relive the feelings we may have run away from then, we see that in a sense, consciously reliving that past is necessary to removal of our emotional blocks. We see also that feelings from the past will continue to haunt us until we do allow them to surface so we can stop avoiding them. Instead, we face them, consciously go through them, then let go of them and go on with our lives. It is as if when we let our unconsciously imprisoned feelings out, they are freed and thereby, we ourselves are freed. Our ego can give up much of the energy it was using in keeping these "horrible" feelings out of our consciousness, and get on with more important tasks in our lives by accepting guidance from our Higher Power.

All of this can be an extremely painful process. It can lead our ego to face its nothingness, which can produce stark terror in us. But when we remember that our ego is only a small part of us, and its nothingness feels so real only because we are so strongly identified with ego, we go through the nothingness and begin to realize our "everythingness" as a child of an Infinite God in a very humble way. If we wish to end the pain and suffering, our ego must be tamed to the point where it becomes willing to cooperate in accepting the guidance of our Higher Self or Higher Power as transmitted through our "I."

I don't want to leave you with the impression that looking into ourselves always leads to thoughts of suicide or ending our lives. It doesn't. For many of us who may have less deeply insane egos, the pain may not be nearly so excruciating and for a few, there may be little or no pain at all. The point is, that we gain nothing from envying someone else who may be having an easier time than we. That also slows us down because *we proceed with the greatest speed when we accept who we are and where we are.* We start from there and go one step at a time through the process of self-examination and house-cleaning. Envy, jealousy, or wishing we were different are more ego escapes to slow down or stop the process by causing us to lose track of who we are, and to avoid doing the work we need to do to find out. There comes a time when our ego learns that any further protection it tries to give us against finding the truth will lead to our joint destruction, rather than the reconstruction we so desperately need.

Having gone to a certain depth in the "inventory" process — different for each of us, our ego becomes ready to accept the help of our "I" in making the decision, "I will not kill myself, no matter what; I am willing to continue this life to its natural conclusion and to go through, with the help of God, whatever I must to reach the truth. I realize I must do it myself because the pain, anger, guilt, and shame I have gone through are the result of *my* ego's mistakes which I need to correct with the help of my Higher Power. I learn to trust my infinitely loving God more every day, realizing that since I'm a part of Him, created by Him, and He is within me, He will not do anything to harm me. That would be harming Himself — something which is not within His nature. Through this growing trust, I turn myself and my ego over to the care of this loving God completely so that I may be guided by His Divine Will, always."

We cannot say and feel this prayer until we are truly ready, and no one can tell us when that is. But, if we diligently and patiently continue the work of looking into the years of amassed deceptions of our ego; if we continue to recognize and accept our ego's resistance as long as necessary, we will come to a point where our ego is ready to surrender enough to make this conscious and unconscious decision to place our lives entirely in the care of the Higher Power within us. We will then make this decision, and on the other side of it, find freedom.

Chapter 11
Acceptance and Gratitude

Acceptance is both very helpful to the process of looking into ourselves and almost a necessity to carrying it out successfully. It is one of the hardest qualities to learn because it is opposed to the desires of the ego.

Since the ego keeps insisting on as absolute control as it can get, it wants no part of acceptance. Acceptance to the ego is akin to surrender which it sees as equivalent to submission. The ego doesn't want to accept anything that isn't in accord with its own will. It wants to make everything and everyone conform to its desires — yet it will not conform with anything or anyone if it can help it. Failing that, it will conform to the hilt, and resent, rage at, and hate the authority it conforms to. Many of us experience our ego's insantiy as a repeated vascillation between these two extremes.

Acceptance comes very slowly and very hard to the ego, but sooner or later, it does come. Sometimes the ego has to create a great deal of pain for itself and others before it realizes that the pain of accepting is far less than the pain of continued fighting.

Acceptance means taking and receiving ourselves, other people, and circumstances in our lives exactly as they are, and feeling OK about it. It also means letting go of the things we cannot do anything about and realizing all will be well even if our ego doesn't control everything. In fact, as we gradually learn to accept, we come to know that our lives greatly improve when our ego doesn't control them. But it takes a while to get to this degree of acceptance.

A good way to start accepting is to learn and repeat to ourselves the well-known Serenity Prayer until its practice and application become a central part of our lives.

> God, grant me the Serenity
> To *accept* the things I cannot change,
> Courage to change the things I can,
> And Wisdom to know the difference.

This is the first and best known part of an age-old prayer which has helped countless numbers of us to learn acceptance and to differentiate it from submission, humiliation, and disgrace.

The first part of the prayer tells us that we need only accept the things we cannot change. It also tells us that to accept those things, we need some measure of serenity, and finally the prayer makes it clear that the only place we can obtain this serenity is from God. That's why we ask Him to grant it. Our ego cannot give us or bring us serenity because its thing is to fight, influence, or force things and people to change. Thereby, it creates chaos within ourselves and others. So we must come to a point where the ego becomes willing to surrender so we can turn away from it as a source of direction, and toward our Higher Power or God within us. Only here can we find the measure of serenity we need to begin to accept what we cannot change.

To know whether we can change something or not, we must have made some effort to change it. In the second part, the prayer suggests that we ask God for the courage we need to do that. The third part of the prayer proposes that we also ask God for the wisdom necessary to know the difference between the things we can and cannot change. This is to avoid expending a great deal of energy trying to change things that cannot be changed, only to find this out through hard and bitter experience. Also, equipped with this wisdom, we will be less likely to let opportunities go by without attempting to change some things that we could change fairly easily if we were just willing to try.

Perhaps to be most efficient, the prayer should be reversed. We should first ask God to grant us the wisdom to know the difference between the things we can change and those we can't. Next, ask for the courage to change the things we can which we have determined through the wisdom He has given us; and finally ask for the serenity to *accept* all that is left — the things we cannot change.

The serenity prayer is especially helpful when we're looking into ourselves. The prayer teaches us that we can't change our past, but we can accept it. If we are willing, we can change the way we view our past, and the way we feel about it and about ourselves. In fact, the way we see our past can greatly help us to accept it. If we had difficult experiences in childhood during which we repressed many feelings, we can begin to appreciate how these locked-up feelings affect our reactions to current situations. We can begin to let those feelings out slowly, in safe constructive ways, rather than continue to be a slave to the destruction of pent-up feelings which grow and fester within us. Acceptance really helps to make this process easier.

Acceptance of ourselves is giving up criticism, judgment, or condemnation of ourselves for anything we may have done or even anything we may be doing now. It is giving up the wish to be any different than we are at this moment. It is beginning to feel OK with, and then to like, and eventually to love the parts of ourselves that our ego wants to reject with anger and hatred. Anger and hatred aggravate the problem or condition we experience. Acceptance and love heal it and transform it into a beautiful, creative expression of ourselves as children of our Creator. All love and infinite acceptance come from God, Who is within ourselves. So to begin practicing acceptance, we stop identifying with the negativity of our ego, and begin to identify with the God consciousness within us. As we do this, God, through our "I," gives us all the help we ask for.

We need to learn that *nothing within us changes unless we first accept it.* As long as our ego continues to reject any part of ourselves, including itself, it will continue to clamor for attention in destructive ways until we pay attention and give it the love and acceptance it asks for and deserves. It's like the myth of the frog which, when kissed by the fair maiden, turns into a handsome prince; or the legend of beauty and the beast. When beauty truly loves the beast, he is freed from his ugliness and turns into a handsome prince who offers her his kindgom. As long as we turn away from the frogs and the beasts within us, they keep growing more warts and become bigger monsters. When we turn and face the frog or the monster, and kiss it, embrace it, and learn to love it, it suddenly changes into a "handsome prince." For the men among us, there is a similar myth about an ugly, old witch, who when kissed by the knight, turns into a beautiful and fair princess.

Acceptance helps us to learn to love the ugly, forlorn, unwanted, crippled, rageful, hateful parts of us that we don't even know exist inside us. The ego says, "Out of sight, out of mind," and adds, "Out of mind, out of existence;" and we believe it. But this is just another of the ego's self-protective lies. Again, it protects itself at our expense. As we accept these forsaken parts of us, they no longer need to act out in ways that are destructive to ourselves and others. We find we become more loving and, therefore, more lovable to those around us toward whom we may have been hostile or rejecting. We realize we're all tied together by a spiritual bond so strong that no outward appearance or inner monsters can touch it. We come to know that we are truly on our way to God.

Gratitude is another very helpful attitude we need to develop if we wish to advance our progress toward greater spiritual awareness. Gratitude helps us to become more accepting, and cultivating acceptance helps gratitude to grow within us. The two qualities are mutually enhancing.

Since the ego never wants to feel indebted to anyone and insists on believing itself to be self-sufficient even when it is terribly dependent, it knows little about gratitude. In fact, to the ego, gratitude is tantamount to indebtedness, subservience, and even groveling. The feeling of gratitude requires a certain degree of humility on our part. But the ego's way is arrogance: "I can do it myself; I don't need anyone. Leave me alone."

The ego doesn't arrive at this isolated place by chance or accident. It arrives there as a result of its own unrealistic expectations about how the world should run. Expecting everyone to fall in with its way of being and doing things, the ego sets itself up for disappointment time after time. After enough of these, it wants to shove everyone away, and insists on, "I'll do it myself." This is another self-protection against further hurt which backfires. It creates the much deeper hurt of isolation, separation, and eventually, self-hate.

As we begin to feel the beneficial effects of the clearing out and airing out process which occurs as we look into ourselves with increasing acceptance, we begin to feel grateful that we have found a way to let our "monsters" and "demons" loose before they destroyed us and others around us. As our growth process continues, and our resentments, fears, and guilts are removed, we realize one day that we are grateful to be alive. More and more "reasons" to be grateful begin to emerge. We begin to concentrate more attention on our assets than our liabilities. When we begin to see how liabilities are turned into assets by our Higher Power, we see that there are *no* permanent liabilities. We see that what we call a liability can become the very bedrock upon which we build strength and new capabilities. All we need is to be willing to tune our minds to the spiritual frequencies of our inner, all-pervasive God instead of concentrating our energy on the defects of our ego or what may be missing within us.

Those of us who have all our physical faculties can feel grateful for every one of our limbs, our organs, our senses, our fingers and toes. Those of us who have one or more of these missing can set about learning to reorient our values so that we place less emphasis on the physical, and more on the essential nature of the spiritual being we truly are, which underlies and upholds all that is physical. Even if we're completely immobilized by paralysis or lack of arms and legs, we can learn to surmount our apparent "handicaps" and feel grateful that we have a mind and a brain which we can train to function to help others and to serve God and our fellows according to His will rather than our ego's will. No matter how heavy we may think our cross is to bear, there are those who are bearing a heavier one. We can feel grateful that we can breathe, that we can enjoy the sights, sounds, or smells of nature, the birds, the crickets, the ocean waves, a bubbling brook, the smell of flowers.

Gratitude is a quality of mind and heart we can practice. The more we practice it, the better at it we become. The more we turn our thoughts to giving thanks for what we have been given, the more we seem to have. We begin to realize that everything we are and everything we have is a gift of God which has been given us out of His infinite goodness, generosity, and grace.

We come to see that since we are the created children of an all-loving God, He loves us all equally with all the love that He has and is, which is infinite. Since we are all integral parts of Him, when he gives to us, He really gives to Himself. Our true nature and essence *is* God. Only our egos are not God because they have arisen to fill the gap created by our misuse of the free will He gave us.

It takes a great deal of humility to feel gratitude for all of God's gifts. Many of us are still too identified with the arrogance, hidden self-abasement, and separation of our egos to be able to recognize and realize the abundance of our Higher Power. Our unconscious egos set up limitations to the flow of God's infinite abundance without realizing that it's our own ego's negative beliefs that are impeding the flow. Our ego believes that, "You don't get something for nothing." Because of its economic/industrial conditioning, our ego interprets this to mean that we have to pay either in money or work for everything we get. It cannot believe that God has free gifts for all of us in infinite abundance which we can manifest in our lives when we align our consciousness with God's; that is when we get out of our ego and let our "I" guide us toward the God within us. The only requirement to receive all that He has is to use what we receive to help our fellow human beings.

When our ego surrenders and we turn our will and our lives over to the care of God, as we understand Him, we slowly become filled with gratitude, acceptance, willingness, humility, and eventually love for ourselves, for our fellows and for God. Our ego barriers appear to fall away as God removes them. Our good begins its natural flow from God to us and we become evermore grateful to be a child and creation of such a loving, caring parent. We begin to know what it means to be "as a little child." We realize that with all our intelligence, with all the knowledge our ego has acquired, we actually know very little. And much of what we do know are lies and distortions of our ego.

We learn that we must unlearn a great deal, if not all, that we have previously learned. We find that we are now in a different kind of school where knowledge comes not only from books others have written or words other people speak to us, but also from inside ourselves. Through prayer and meditation we develop our intuition which is a channel through which we learn directly the infinite knowledge God already knows. We begin to pay more attention to impressions, senses, and other ways God tries to communicate with us through intuition. We learn that intuition must be developed through practice, just as bicycle riding or tennis playing must. We eventually realize that our intuition is another of the limitless gifts God has for us if we're willing to receive it.

We begin to see giving and receiving as gifts of God too, that our ego has been preventing us from accepting. Many of us have never learned to give freely, as God gives, and to receive openly, as God awaits to receive our love and gratitude. Our ego has always looked at giving and receiving with strings attached. Some of us who have been "people pleasers" much of our lives realize that we really have been trying to please our egos. We have tried to give to please others, but only because our ego expected love, approval, or acceptance in return. When the people we tried to please didn't give us those things, which only God can give, we became disappointed, angry, resentful, and we stopped giving and pleasing those people. Instead, we became withholding, and our relationships soured. Eventually they ended. Our ego, then, immediately set about repeating the same pattern with new people — new relationships or a group of new "friends."

Now that we're on a path of spiritual development which includes becoming more aware of the presence of God as our Source and Constant Companion, and engaging in the difficult task of removing our ego's inner barriers to our acceptance of God, we see that the only true giving is giving with no strings of any kind attached. This is giving from our Spirit which expects and needs nothing in return because sheer joy results from this kind of giving. It is not bargaining, negotiating, or manipulating. It is not giving to get something back. It's simply the free, generous giving of ourselves to each other and to God in the same way God gives to us.

As the meaning of true giving dawns on our consciousness, we realize that we can also openly receive from God and from other human beings without feeling an obligation or a duty to repay. We can truly receive because we are children of an infinitely loving God who asks nothing in return except that we be happy, joyous, peaceful, caring of each other, and as fully expressive of His love and caring for us as we can possibly be. We realize that we're all bound to our Father/Mother and to each other by a bond of love so strong that it can never be broken, never has been, and never will be. In this bond of love, we find freedom. For this kind of gift, who can help but feel grateful?

Chapter 12
Forgiveness and Humility

As we continue the work of looking into ourselves, we become more and more honest. The deceptions of our ego fall away one by one, and we begin to accept who we really are. We begin to see how we (our egos) have been responsible for our own lot in life, how we have played a major part in creating every situation we used to blame everyone else for. We become more accepting of ourselves and we learn to be good to ourselves. We find that the more we can be good to ourselves, the better we feel about ourselves and who we are. Our self-acceptance improves and our self-esteem goes up.

When, through awareness of the Higher Power within us and honesty about the errors and deviations of our egos, we begin to see that the path to peace and joy is one of gentle patience and perseverence, we also begin to see that humility and forgiveness have much to offer in furthering the process of healing.

Forgiveness and humility are the means our Higher Power uses through our "I" to get our ego to let go of its resentments. As we mentioned, resentments or grudges constitute the prime tool of separation and isolation of an overblown, over-sensitive ego. As soon as someone doesn't act as our ego thinks they should (they don't smile at us; they ignore us; they walk away from us, slight us, or in any way act rejecting toward us), the ego responds with instant anger generated not only by the person's current behavior, but reinforced by all the accumulated unconscious resentments our ego has stored up from *similar* imagined "insults" in the past. This anger may vary in intensity from mild annoyance to furious, red-hot rage. If we don't allow ourselves to feel this anger, let alone express it, it turns into an ongoing resentment of which we may be conscious or unconscious. If we are conscious of it, we say, "I hate that person; he has hurt me and I will hurt him back," or "I will stay away from him so I won't be hurt again." Or we may say, "I can't stand that person; every time I get around her, I end up getting hurt or upset." So we isolate ourselves from one more person and go on harboring our resentment. If this happens too many times, our resentments may eventually turn into depression and a feeling that the world is out to get us.

If we are not conscious of our resentments, matters become even worse. We may smile at the person and act sweetly, perhaps even calling that person and others "honey" and "sweetie," while under all the surface sweetness lurks the anger and resentment waiting to strike at the first reasonably "safe" opportunity (often the wrong person at the wrong time, for the wrong reason). Rather than strike out directly, our ego may resort to indirect expressions of hostility such as snide or cutting remarks, sarcasm, subtle put-downs expressed in a "joking" manner, or even milder forms such as forgetting something important to another person — the time of an appointment, the person's name, a birthday, etc.

Whether conscious or unconscious, the damage of our ego's resentments is done to us rather than the person we resent. The resentment is the ego's way to bolster its protective position which blocks the way to finding our inner Higher Power and the consequent peace, joy, and freedom which comes from our Inner Source. Our ego's resentments keep us trapped like prisoners in a cage. The only way we can experience true freedom, lightness, and joy is to walk the path leading toward our spiritual center or Higher Power. To experience this freedom, we keep moving *unhurriedly* on this path. To do this, we continue the work of uncovering our resentments so they can be transformed by our "I" into constructive, friendly energy. These resentments are hidden roadblocks within us. They can't be removed if we don't honestly uncover them, humbly accept them as our own, and prepare ourselves fully to turn them over to the care of our Higher Power.

Partly because of all the resentments it harbors, the ego also believes that it is "bad," no matter how much it tries to tell us and the world otherwise. It doesn't feel deserving of the abundance of God; it isn't entitled to have it. To reinforce this unbelief, the ego doesn't allow itself to believe that God has any such abundance; or that if He does, He would just go around giving it out freely to everyone. The ego is willing to believe that God may lavish His abundance on some chosen few; but certainly not on everyone. Just look at all the hungry people in the world, the ego says.

It is true that all of us who have wandered away from God and replaced Him with our own egos have allowed these egos to do much that has been "bad" for us and others. It is also true that this has resulted in greater apparent separation from our Source and our Home. But it is *not* true that we have to suffer for our so-called "sins" forever and ever. We suffer only while we still err. There comes a time when we see the error of our ego's ways, we hit a "bottom," and make a decision to come out of the darkness and follow the light of God. Since God is infinitely forgiving, our errors are already forgiven even before we hit our bottom. God has always loved us with an unconditional, unlimited love greater than that of any mother for her child. It is we who suffer from the guilt of our ego's deeds, conscious or unconscious, and keep ourselves away from our infinitely loving Father/Mother because we feel unworthy.

Two of the tools we use to help our Higher Power accomplish the miracle of freeing us from our ego are forgiveness and humility. These go together, hand in hand. We cannot forgive anyone without some degree of humility, and we cannot become humble if we unforgivingly hang on to our righteous indignation, anger, resentment or even fear, guilt, and shame.

It is so hard for so many of us to learn to forgive because our ego knows that do to this, it must give up its position of imagined strength and self-protection. To learn the lesson of forgiveness, we must allow time for the ego's defenses to weaken. We need to give our ego the time and let it suffer the pain that it needs to eventually soften up. Many of us ask, "Why must I suffer so? Why is growth so painful?" *Growth is not painful. It is our ego's resistance to growth that causes the pain.* Our ego is often unwilling to surrender without pain. Pain is the price it demands for giving up its insane, destructive ways and learning a new and better way. The only way I know not to have any pain is not to have an ego, or to have a fully surrendered ego. Since our ego is the only part of us that suffers, and it creates its own suffering, if we didn't have an ego (or if all egos were surrendered,) there would be no suffering — no fear, no pain, no guilt, no depression, no paranoia, no illness or disease of any kind. There would be no crime, no wars, no conflicts, no fights. All of these are products of the ego when it is allowed to have its way. It is almost impossible for us to imagine what a world without ego would be like. It would be the Kingdom of God on earth; it would be heaven.

So our pain is our ego's way of learning that its own resistance is the cause of pain and that its surrender is the release from pain. When we accept our pain, that is, accept that *our* ego is causing and perpetuating it, not someone else's, we begin to gain enough humility to learn to forgive. The road to forgiveness passes through humility and the road to humility begins at acceptance. Acceptance is what we do when we surrender — when we realize that fighting will get us nowhere except to more turmoil, more pain, more conflict. Attack begets counter-attack. Revenge fuels counter-revenge and these both lead to escalation of conflicts into major disasters. It's unfortunate that many of our egos will not learn any other way.

To reverse the course of the crazed ego, we learn to forgive. At first, we do the nearly impossible. We ask God, as we understand Him, to bless those who we feel have wronged us. Since our ego's resentment is usually great when someone appears to do us "wrong," this is extremely hard to do. Our ego's automatic response may be one of attack, "I'll get my revenge; I'll fix you; you'll pay me for this!" Or it may be one of indignation, "Why should I be the one to surrender — the one to forgive? She should apologize to me first." The response may also be one of self-pity. "Poor me! Why do all these terrible things happen to me? Why are people so mean to me? What did I do to deserve this?" But if we're willing, we can learn gradually to stop these self-destructive responses of our ego. All we need is a little willingness to see ourselves and our hurt another way.

Instead of identifying so completely with our ego, the only part of us that can be hurt because it is the only part that recognizes and feels hurt, we realize that the true "I" within us is closely allied with God who is also within us. When we identify with this true "I" even for a moment, our ego has lost its hold on us and we can begin to bless a person even though our ego may feel that person has done us wrong. Even if we start by saying, "Bless the S.O.B.," we are accomplishing a part of the ego release necessary to move to a better place. As we do this, we find after a while that we can drop the "S.O.B." part. As we continue this practice, the most wonderful thing happens. We become less ego-bound. Our "I" is free to do its transformative work. We begin to feel better. Much of our anger toward the person we are blessing, and eventually others, abates or disappears completely. Our identification with our Higher Power as a child of God grows, and we experience an increasing sense of serenity, well-being and eventually, love.

Since our egos do as much damage to ourselves as to others by keeping us from the realization of who we truly are, which is the God within us, we need to learn to be forgiving toward our own ego. Again, we need to learn to be good to ourselves and gentle with ourselves. We need to learn to stop criticizing, chastising and condemning ourselves for not being perfect, or not making enough progress fast enough. By identifying more and more with the God within us, we learn to stop feeling inferior and unworthy. We recognize those feelings as being those of our ego — not of God. As each of us realizes that he or she is a son or daughter of God, we come to know that our rightful place is within our Father where we continually share in all the love, peace, joy, and abundance that He IS.

Eventually, as we come to love ourselves more, we realize that there is nothing we or anyone else has done that needs to be forgiven. When we see that we're all here doing the best we can, learning as best we can, we can stop putting judgments on ourselves and others for their words, deeds, or behavior. We can stop seeing ourselves as victims of terrible oppressors. We can stop fearing our "paper tigers." We see that we have nothing to fear except the parts of us our egos still haven't allowed us to see. When these "terrible" parts of us are exposed to the light of our loving Higher Power, they indeed turn into the "paper tigers" they really are.

We come to know that the same God that is in us is in every individual soul, and that God in all of us is obscured and blocked by our overblown, oversized ego. We learn slowly and often painfully that our task here on earth is to learn to detach our identity from our egos so that we may find and identify with our true Self which is God. Our eyes (inner eyes) are slowly opened and we come to know that no one is keeping God's infinite good from us but our own ego and its unwillingness to forgive. We begin to understand that the path from ego to God must go through forgiveness and eventually lead to a place where forgiveness becomes unnecessary because there is nothing to forgive. In this place, we truly let go of our ego's hurts, fears, and needs for revenge. We feel closer to others as we give up the separateness our ego has so long maintained. We realize that separateness is the result of our own ego's resentments, grudges, and often unexpressed rage. *We come to know that we must admit, own, and possibly live through all of that within ourselves before we can truly let go of it.* Those resentments, angers and rages are what our ego uses to maintain its hold on us. As soon as we decide we don't want to play the ego's games anymore, we improve. As soon as we're ready to give up being right, getting revenge, and making sure things are always "fair," we win because then we are out of our ego and into our "I" where we can forgive. We need to continue to forgive and forgive and forgive ourselves and others until we reach the point where we recognize that no wrong is being done or can be done to us. At that point, we will realize that we cannot do any wrong to anyone else, and forgiveness will become unnecessary. We will have outgrown it.

We need to realize that the games the ego plays of attack, revenge and defense, even if we allow them to go on only in our heads, are destructive for us. They cause us to feel more alone and more self-hateful because when we hate or hurt another person, we cannot help but hate and hurt ourselves. This occurs because of the spiritual bond which exists between all of us. The ego will deny this vehemently, but it is true nevertheless. One thing we become more certain of during this process of transformation is that anything the ego says is a lie, and the more strongly the ego hangs on to a belief, the more false it is.

Chapter 13
Prayer and Meditation

From the very beginning of our spiritual transformation, we benefit greatly by learning to pray and meditate regularly. Our prayers are not something God demands or requires or needs from us. They are our way of contacting the God part of ourselves through the defenses of our ego. Both prayer and meditation open channels to our inner Higher Power. They loosen the grasp of our ego on our consciousness so that our "I" can be free to perform the miracles of transformation.

It is not surprising that there is a great deal of confusion about both prayer and meditation because they are so foreign to the ego's nature. There is no "right" way to do them. Both are experimental at our own individual level. Hopefully the few pointers I can offer in this chapter will help to reduce some of the confusion.

Each of us does need to find a way that suits her or him best. We can do this by listening to how others do it and have done it for ages immemorial, and pick what seems helpful to us, try it out, and see what happens. Not what happens in terms of material results or quick changes, but more what happens in terms of our increased serenity, improved health, our life going more smoothly than it used to, our relationships with our fellow human beings improving over a prolonged time period. These are the real results of meditation rather than how much money we get, how many material things we have, or whether we are promoted at work or get a new job. It's not that material things are unimportant, but that if we pray for these alone, we're really missing the point and short-changing ourselves. The point seems to be that when we align our consciousness with that of the Higher Power within us — when our ego begins to surrender as we begin to see that we're not all ego — when the "I" we identify with begins to shift from ego to God, then we open ourselves to receive all the material things God has to give us. As He helps us literally to materialize exactly what we need when we need it, we begin to trust that the God within us knows better than we do what we need materially. Only our egos keep us from our good, not God. God wants each of us to have all of what He has — which is Infinite — because He is infinitely loving and giving. His supply of everything is unlimited because whatever He needs, He creates as He always has and always will. He always has exactly enough for all of us because He knows no such thing as lack or want. Those are ego inventions and they are as false as everything the ego invents.

As we learn to believe this more and more, deep down at the bottom of our hearts, it begins to materialize for us. When we doubt or don't believe, we stop God's infinite flow of ongoing creation for us. We say, "No, not for me; it cannot be. What have I done to earn such bountiful goodness?" The answer seems to be that we need "do" nothing but accept that we are God's children and realize or remember what that means. It means that God's ability to create whatever is needed is unlimited as is everything about Him. He has created the universe including billions of galaxies containing trillions of suns and planets. On at least one of these planets, but probably many more, He has created majestic mountains; vast oceans; rich, fertile fields; bountiful minerals; a myriad species of plants and animals; and us. Through us, He has created innumerable things which are what we call material and physical, and He continues to create because creation never stops.

But all these material things begin as a push toward Life, which is the energy of God. This push toward Life expresses itself as dreams, ideas, and thoughts in the individual minds of human beings who, themselves, are individual expressions of the One and Only Mind of God. By truly realizing our Oneness with God, that our individual minds are united in His and comprise His Mind, we become able to create as God creates because He has given us all that He IS, including the ability to create.

Our egos, however, do not and cannot believe this, although it is happening all the time. Our egos make use of God's ability to create — which He has given us — on a daily basis. But our egos create, not according to the freedom God has given us, but according to the limitations they have made up. Our egos believe that to create a loaf of bread, grain must be sown and harvested in the field, wheat must be separated from chaff and ground to a fine flour, dough must be made from the flour, yeast must be added, and the whole thing must be baked in an oven for a certain time. When we grow beyond the limitations of our egos, and identify with our true "I" which is of God, we will know how to create bread by extending our hand when the bread is needed, and the bread will materialize in our hand.

The same is true about any other material object we may need. The ego believes that to move over great distances, we need cars, ships, and planes; so it creates and manufactures them. But our "I" knows that when we rise beyond the limitations our ego insists on believing in, we can transport ourselves and our bodies instantly to any place on earth or in the universe where we may need to go. In other words, as incredulous as it may sound to our egos, we need create according to the ego's limited and laborious ways only so long as we continue to believe that we're restricted by those limited inventions of our own egos.

To prove this cannot be true, our egos have set up barriers in our minds which cut us off from God. We forget our true Divine, eternal, spiritual nature, and become used to thinking, feeling, and acting like mortal egos in physical bodies. We learn to believe more in the limited, negative, imaginary laws of the ego, and forget that we are all part of the infinite Essence of God. We forget to see ourselves as individual manifestations of the One and Only, All-Encompassing God. We become convinced by the lies our egos tell us, that we are separate beings in separate bodies, living in a cold, cruel, limited, competitive, material world. All this seems so real to us that we cannot believe it isn't. We can't believe that our true nature is spiritual and that there is only One Spirit which includes and protects us all, if we only recognize and embrace Him.

When we pray to realize that we are one with Him Who created us, our prayers serve to remind us of the Infinite Nature within each of us. This kind of prayer seems most helpful in gently keeping our ego in line so that the probability of our thinking it's doing it all (pride and arrogance) will be minimized. The chance that our ego will become angry if it doesn't get the results *it* wants are minimized as well.

This kind of prayer is a big jump for most of us from the childhood prayers we begin with. "Be a good boy or girl, or God will punish you," may still often ring in our ears. Many of us may even repeat it to our children. Even if we don't, it may be tucked away in our subconscious ego, controlling our beliefs without our being aware of it. Before we can graduate to the most effective form of prayer, we may have to let go of many old, outmoded, untrue beliefs about God. We may have to come to see Him as an Entity or Energy that can only love, support, create, sustain, and bring joy rather than judge, condemn or punish. We may have to let go of our old concepts of heaven and hell as separate places where the good and bad people go after death, respectively. We may need to come to realize that good and bad are judgments of the ego, not of God; that heaven and hell are states of mind we manufacture ourselves right here on earth and probably after the death of our bodies, too, depending upon our beliefs and attitudes, and our identification with our ego or our Higher Power.

When we identify with our ego, we feel alone, separate, inadequate, or worthless. This is truly a hell of our own making. As our true identity emerges from the shackles of our ego, and our "I" begins to work consciously, we begin to recognize that the Higher Power within each of us is not some super-ego in disguise that is going to trick us into believing and trusting It so It can bash us over the head with a large club. We recognize this suspicion as more obstructionistic work of our ego. We come to know that our Higher Power doesn't create to destroy; He creates to enjoy. He creates us to enjoy us and for us to enjoy Him and all the rest of His creations. We are not separate and alone. Spiritually we are all One with Him and all His creations. As we allow these truths to become our consciousness, we become ready to enter the Kingdom of Heaven.

When we begin to get a glimmer of this, no matter how dim, we can humbly pray, "God, Father/Mother, here I am, your humble child and servant, here to do Your will which is also my will, and opposite to my ego's will. Please help me to tame my ego so that I may become more accepting of my Oneness with You — so that I may realize that we have never been apart — but that my ego has created the illusion of our separateness. Deep in my heart, I want to know my Oneness with You with all my being because I know that is the Truth for You.

"We human beings are all Your children. We have manufactured runaway egos which have strayed from Your path. Yet we know You love us with a love we can only dimly experience. We know You see our egos' crimes and sins — if you see them at all — only as errors to be corrected so that we may realize we are still One with You. We want with all our hearts to be in our rightful places in You, and we know that as we accept Your all-generous help with gratitude and humility, that will happen. We wish we could come to our Oneness with You faster but realize our egos need time to let go of their mistakes, to change their false beliefs, and to make the 180-degree turn we need to begin moving toward You. Thank You, Father/Mother, for all Your loving help." I suggest reading this prayer slowly several times, especially when feeling troubled.

As I pointed out in Chapter 3, meditation is an important process which helps us contact the Higher Power within us. Our ego doesn't understand the need for meditation, nor does it want to. It senses that our meditating will allow our "I" to emerge and this will lead to the end of the ego's control over our lives. This is the prime and greatest fear of the ego: loss of control. This is why the ego is so afraid of death. Under the fear of death which is commonly accepted as the ego's greatest fear, lurks the fear of losing control. The ego knows it cannot control what happens beyond the body's death. It can only control us here, while we are in physical bodies, and even here, for only as long as we allow it. Even though our soul — our "I" and part of our ego — may continue beyond the habitation of a physical body, the evidence seems to indicate that, for most of us, our "I," the wise/God part of our soul, takes over after our body's death and guides the evaluation process which takes place then. The ego's chance to control disappears or at least is greatly diminished compared to what it is while in the physical state.

So meditation is threatening and frightening to the ego. It invents all kinds of reasons why we shouldn't do it. The ego tells us, "Meditation is silly; it doesn't work; it leads to being lazy and shiftless." Our ego puts words in our mouths and beliefs in our heads like, "I can't sit still; I can't see any results. Meditation makes me uncomfortable. What good can come from something where you just sit and *do* nothing?" The ego is so performance- and production-oriented that it can see no value in the quiet stillness necessary for entering the void where God may be consciously experienced. Because of its fear of these, the ego sees only negative value in any attempt to meditate.

As usual, what the ego wants is the opposite of that which is in our best interest as well as the best interest of everyone else. We need to learn to recognize that in many areas, when in doubt, do the opposite of what our ego is telling us. So, in spite of all the ego's protestations, if we wish to reduce our pain and struggle, and increase our feeling of peace, freedom, and joy, we need to learn to meditate on a regular basis. But we must learn slowly and gently. As we know, we can't coerce or brute force our ego. It fights back and slows or stymies our progress.

Meditation is a process we begin by relaxing and quieting our bodies, then go on to allowing our minds to become quiet, our thoughts to slow down, diminish, and eventually, perhaps after a long term of practice, to cease altogether. When this happens, we are in true contact with the Higher Power within us.

The key to meditation is to *let* it happen rather than to *make* it happen or force it to happen. As in all spiritual matters, *letting* works much better and faster than making or forcing. Of course, "letting" is not the ego's way. When the ego sees that it cannot win against our quiet determination to learn to meditate, it flips to the other extreme of *making* it happen *now!* When it can't do that, it uses this inability as proof that we're no good at it. We will *never* learn, the ego says, so why try at all? Might as well give up.

The antidote to these ego barriers seems to be to acknowledge our ego's resistance without putting ourselves or our ego down, and to persist gently but firmly in spite of this resistance. Eventually, our body quiets down. We stop shifting, twitching, and itching, and we are able to relax for increasing periods of time. As we let the energy drain out of our bodies, we allow our thoughts to slow down. We enter into the realm of peace and quiet — the realm of God.

This process of quieting ourselves has to be learned. As our ego does all in its power to activate our minds with all kinds of ideas and thoughts, we learn to observe these thoughts. We don't try to stop them, but we *let* them through without becoming attached to them and following them. This is not easy. it requires a great deal of patience and humility. We build these gradually through repeating the process of quieting ourselves day in and day out. We experience progress and retardation. But if we keep practicing, we improve slowly, one day at a time.

One purpose of meditation is to teach our minds to concentrate. Because our minds are such wanderers, flitting from one thought to the next with great apparent agility, they must be taught to slow down and concentrate on one thing. For those who are word- or sound-oriented, the object of concentration may be a mantrum or chant, repeated over and over. Those who are more visually oriented may prefer an image held in their awareness of a pleasant sight, such as a sunset, a vase of flowers, or a bowl of fruit. Later, a single flower or piece of fruit may be used. The object may start to move or revolve. Let it do what it will while merely observing it with relaxed concentration.

Some people concentrate on counting their breaths and noticing the air as it enters and leaves their nostrils. A whole system of Yoga called Kriya Yoga is based on the breath and includes breathing exercises. Hatha Yoga, the Yoga of body movement also includes breathing control. Breath is the vital energy of physical life. As such, it is a link between the spiritual and the physical. It may be thought of as the means through which the spiritual energy of life is brought into our bodies to animate them. Stop the breath, and the body quickly dies. The word "spirit" comes from the Latin "spire" which is to breathe. To inspire means both to take in breath and to let God's ideas enter our consciousness.

The *letting* of meditation is also closely related to waiting — waiting for something to happen without knowing what it is. This is where patience must combine with faith that if we continue this practice, something beneficial will happen. We learn to wait patiently, giving up any thought of how long it will take or how quickly it will happen. We learn to let our "I" receive the impatience of our ego and transform it into faith that at just the right time, we will begin to sense or feel something. It may be an all-pervasive sense of peace — a serenity such as we have not known before, or a feeling that everything is right with the world; everything is exactly as it is meant to be — in its proper place at the proper time. Our sense of space and/or time may disappear, being replaced by a sense of active, alert, suspended animation — an effortless floating in a timeless universe.

Some people may experience being separated from their bodies for brief periods of time. Such experiences are described by Robert Monroe in *Journeys Out of the Body* and by Charles Tart and others who are attempting to study these experiences in a scientific manner.

If your meditation experience gives rise to some degree of fear within you, don't be alarmed. It may be that you have temporarily wandered too far beyond the boundaries where your ego is comfortable at your stage of development. Try to continue for a while if the fear is not too great to see if it will subside. Realize that when you're close to that inner Higher Power within you, there is nothing to fear, but that your ego doesn't want you to achieve this closeness; so it will try to stop you by any means at its disposal. Fear, of course, is a prime tool of the ego and practically inseparable from it. Where there is ego, there is fear, and the fear is proportionate to the size of the ego.

If after gentle persistence, the fear doesn't subside or grows larger, then stop and realize you will need more preparation before going further. Perhaps you need to retrace some steps already taken, going back to an earlier stage, or perhaps more faith to realize that fears, although appearing and feeling terribly real at times, are always paper tigers which disappear as our faith in our Higher Power grows and our faith in our own ego diminishes.

As I mentioned in Chapter 3, many books on meditation have been written by both Eastern and Western authors. It is not a strange Eastern practice. It has been practiced by all people throughout the world who have been interested in bringing their inner contact with their Higher Power to conscious awareness. Most books on the subject cover such elementary material as posture, position, and location. I won't belabor these here. Suffice it to say that any quiet environment will do to start. Any comfortable, relaxed position will serve, though we seem to get more benefit when our spine is straight and vertical, feet flat on the floor, if sitting in a chair — the legs uncrossed to keep the energy in the two sides of the body separate. The hands may be in your lap with palms facing up. All body parts should be as relaxed as possible. The idea is to assume a position in which you can relax while staying awake and alert. Some people prefer the classical lotus position, which is sitting on the floor, cross-legged. If you use this position, you may want to sit on a meditation mat which you use only for that purpose, as it builds up positive "vibrations" helpful to meditation as you continue to use it.

It's easy for the beginning meditator to fall asleep while meditating. This is OK, but we recognize it as an another avoiding tactic of the ego. If you manage to sneak in a few minutes of relaxation before going to sleep, you may be ahead of the game and on your way. In the upright spine position, it's more difficult to fall asleep than lying down.

After some period of practice — it may be days, weeks, or months — the experience of quiet peace becomes so enjoyable that we no longer drop off to sleep. As we transcend our thoughts, the experience of quiet and peace becomes so soothing and exhilarating at the same time that we look forward to our meditation periods. Paradoxically, they seem to be both energy boosters during the day, and an excellent preparation for sleep at night.

We don't become foggy — or fuzzy-brained as some have feared. These fears are more ego tactics to dissuade us. Those of us who continue the practice despite our ego distractions find eventually a haven, a refuge where we can go to feel safe, to be refreshed and renewed, when the ego world becomes temporarily too heavy to bear. We find that occasional periods of meditation, even if no longer than a minute or two, give us renewed energy with which to go on with our day.

Over a period of time, we become better centered within ourselves, less subject to being blown about by the emotional winds or negative thoughts of our or others' egos. Regular meditation helps us to come closer and closer to the Higher Power within us, thus slowly separating our "I" from control of our ego, and identifying more with our divine nature and origin. As this process continues, we find that we become better integrated. We can become more honest about ourselves and our progress. We see ourselves more realistically as a spiritual being who is part of God, inhabiting a body for brief periods in the fabric of eternity. We realize more and more the reality of the spirit and are able to detach from the unreality of the ego without leaving it. Our whole concept of how the world is and the limitations which our egos impose on us begins to change.

This may sound confusing and possibly frightening to some, but remember that fear is of the ego only. If we're patient, unhurried, accepting of all that we can about ourselves including our fears, the fears gradually diminish. As we slowly continue to approach our Higher Power without striving, pushing or trying to make ourselves go faster, our ego's hold on us decreases and our fears along with it. We truly come to know deep within ourselves what we have always known but didn't know that we knew: that God IS; that we are all part of Him; that as we learn more and more that we are of God and in God, our ego becomes more of an unreal dream or fantasy.

We know that while we're inhabiting the earth in our physical bodies, we need to take care of our ego and our body as our Father/Mother takes care of us, as little children. We finally see and experience the letting go of our ego which means that it need not control us anymore because we, I, have turned to the guidance of my Higher Power. Meditation leads to this place and beyond. It's a gradual, little-at-a-time, cumulative, essential process without which our transformation from ego-bound, limited person to free child of God cannot take place.

Chapter 14
Sharing with Others

Before we start on a spiritual path — a path of transformation from ego to God — we often go to great lengths to avoid sharing ourselves with others. When we're all ego, we're only interested in Number One — ME! We give much lip service to helping others or sharing with them, but usually undertake it only as an obligation or because we're trying to be "good" persons. There's nothing "wrong" with that as such. It's the best we can do at the time. I say this not in a condemning way, but rather as a statement of fact. The ego doesn't like to share or help. It likes to hoard, possess and control. It does these things not because it is inherently evil, but because it is frightened and these are the ways it gives itself the illusion of safety and security. We have seen that fear results from one cause only — our ego's imagined separation from God. I say imagined because *real* separation from God *cannot* exist. We are *never* and can never be separated from God, but our ego can sure imagine that it is, and does so as a matter of course. God is always One, and we are *always* included in Him. Something that is One cannot have separate parts. God is always in us and with us, but our ego doesn't want to hear of, or experience Him. It only wants "I" to be totally it — totally ego.

This imagined separation from God also means separation from our fellow humans. Since God is One and All there is, He includes all His creations so that we cannot be separate. Since God is the Spirit within us, He is within all of us equally. There is not one human being on this earth who can live without the Spirit of God within him or her. Human beings cannot live by ego alone. In fact, they are more likely to die by ego . . . alone. God within us is what keeps us alive. When we allow the awareness and substance of Him to flow freely through us, He not only keeps us alive, but joyous, creative, happy, serene, and loving. We, when identified with our egos, are the ones who block God from flowing and expressing through us.

Further, no one has a better "handle" on God than anyone else. No one has more the ear of God or the Word of God than anyone else. Access to God is available to us all equally if we cooperate in doing the necessary work to open our channels. Since God is in us equally, those of us who have done this work for a while need and want to share with those who have done less or perhaps have not yet consciously started. We need to share with each other as God shares Himself with us whenever we're ready to hear and accept His guidance.

In reality, there are no "others" to share with. We are sharing with ourselves. Since we are all part of the same God, there is only one "I" and that "I" is God. This One I/God has many extensions which are our individual "I"'s. As we begin to differentiate ego from our real "I," we realize that the "new" individual "I" we discover within ourselves, who has always been there, is the bridge between our separate ego and the One God. As we grow in awareness, we recognize this new I more and more as one with God until we arrive at a spiritual level where we fully accept that our "I" is one with God, as it has always been. At that point, ego is completely surrendered. Illusions fall away and all becomes perfect peace, perfect harmony, perfect bliss. When will that happen for us? Most of us cannot predict that because we still have such a long way to travel on the path of spiritual growth. But as we travel together, we realize that we are truly together, traveling to the same place; and by sharing we speed our progress. We help each other along.

It is true that some of us are further along than others in doing the required work to remove our blocks, but who is ahead of whom is not important in the spiritual realm. We are not engaged in a race; only our ego is. Our ego loves to compare our progress with others and then feels good when it thinks it's ahead, and bad when it thinks it's lagging behind. If we allow our ego to take too much control, we may find ourselves zealously and self-righteously "preaching" to those who are not yet ready to hear us. We may develop a "holier-than-thou" attitude. As always, when the ego takes over, the result is anger within those we preach to, and within ourselves for not being heard. This happens to nearly all of us at some point on this path. We need not reprove or punish ourselves for it. We need only recognize these attitudes as ego tactics which impede our progress rather than help it.

We need to become aware that our ego has taken over again; then acknowledge it, really knowing deep within ourselves that it's true. Then we need to ask our Higher Power for enough humility to share with another person what we are doing, and finally become willing to surrender again and humbly continue on our path, helping and cooperating with other parts of God rather than competing with them and comparing our progress with theirs. One true measure of progress, if we need one, is that we no longer need to measure our progress. We no longer need to "show" or prove to anyone how much we know or how far along we are. It's enough for us that we feel it and accept it in humble gratitude.

No matter how much our ego might like to be the first on its block to reach God and unite with

Him (while unconsciously resisting it), we can't do it alone. Because God is One, the process of unification or at-one-ment cannot be complete until all souls or sparks of energy who have strayed have been reunited. So if some of us perform more of the necessary inner work of transformation, and advance further toward the goal than others, we eventually see that our most important work, while allowing our own development to continue, becomes that of helping others by sharing what we learn. In the same way, more "advanced" souls than we, who may no longer need to inhabit physical bodies, "return" from the spirit world to help us. Examples of this type of help abound and will become more accepted in years to come. They have existed from time immemorial. Jesus is a rather familiar example to most of us in this era. He did return to a physical body for a short thirty-three years, but continued to provide our ancestors with tremendous help after the death of that body, and still to this day provides help to millions through many versions of the accounts of His ministry and message, such as found in various editions of the Bible and other spiritual writings. *A Course in Miracles* is one of the most recent examples of these helpful contributions from those no longer in physical form.

Helping and sharing with others is a strong central theme in spiritual development. Though we must each do our own inner work and travel our own individual path through the maze of our own ego digressions, most of us can do this only with the help of the other parts of God and by giving what help we can to those who are ready to receive it. As we continue to grow in awareness of who we truly are, we recognize and accept that we were created by God, that we are His children and creations and that He has never separated Himself from us or cast us out. As this growth of awareness continues, we begin to see how truly puny our "powerful" ego is compared to the majesty and grandeur of God. We begin to see how we have allowed our ego to rob us of the love that God is ready to express through us, and how isolated we have become through the fears of our egos.

As our awareness of the Higher Power within us increases, our blocks to helping other parts of ourselves, other human beings, begin to melt away under the power of love that begins to flow through us. This power of love leads us to true vision of all that God has created and is still creating through us. We see ourselves united with all there is. Our vision of ourselves as separate entities grows dim as we see and experience the strong spiritual bonds of love that unite us. We *naturally* come to want to help, participate, do our part. The world is no longer full of potential enemies waiting at every corner to zap us. The universe is no longer the cold, friendless, lonely place our egos made up. We begin to see the oneness in everything and rejoice in it. We see that we can be one with the world, the universe, and God, not only without losing our individual identity, but while actually enhancing it. We feel an important part of the whole because we know that we are all equal in the eyes of God. There are no special ones because everyone of us is special in his/her own unique way. Under the grace of God, the more we become our own individual "I," the more we become one with the One God that is the only "I." That is the great paradox of individuality within Oneness. We know that we are because God is, and I AM because God IS.

So we learn gradually that sharing is the way to Oneness, and through our sharing we come to a place where we want to give more than we want to receive. We learn that as we give, we also receive in equal measure or greater — never less. We realize that what we share with our fellow parts of God is God Himself, as we have allowed Him to reveal and express Himself through us. When we share God, we are not depleted, we are replenished because God is Infinite and His supply is unlimited.

At the beginning of this sharing, we often feel, "I can't help this person; I have nothing to give."

How true! From our egos alone, we have nothing of value to give. We tend to feel depleted when we try to help someone from our ego resources alone. But when we learn to disidentify from our ego to a greater degree and begin to realize our true divine nature, then we can share by letting God's energy flow through us. He provides the words and actions we need at the time we need them. Then we don't feel depleted, but rather energized and high. The more we let God share Himself through us, the more replenished and united we feel. We experience the safety, security and coziness of true unity. We are united within ourselves, united with our fellows, and united with God. The unity of God has replaced the separateness of ego within us.

Again, we need to be on our guard against the ego's tendency to "grab the ball and run." When we begin to feel some improvement within ourselves, our egos want to run out there and share with the whole world how *we* did it, or even how our Higher Power did it. How quickly we forget the time when we ran as fast as we could from anyone wanting to share their God with us. Our ego tells us we are different. We will not ram it down anyone's throat. We will only share, not thrust! But before we know it, we're talking to anyone who will listen and maybe collaring some who won't. We need to learn to share only with those who ask, and even then, to be sensitive to how ready they are to hear what we have to say.

There was a time when we asked for help and meant, "Give me an answer immediately. Give me an instant solution. Give me a shortcut to end my pain and misery." We were not ready to accept the answer that we had to do our own inner work, no matter how laborious or how long that took. We had to learn to clear our own inner channels to let God's energy flow through us. We had to cooperate in removing enough wreckage of our own past so we could hear the guidance we needed. This wreckage of the past is all the falsities our ego has accumulated for all the years we have been alive — all the lies it has told us about our own nature — that we're inadequate, demanding, domineering, dependent, insensitive, self-centered, and on and on. True, our ego is all of these and more, but our ego isn't our true nature. Our true nature is God and only God, because God is One and Infinite. So God is all there is — including every one of us.

Someone who has not done at least *some* of this inner clearing work and does not yet see the necessity for it, no matter how much she may be hurting, will not be ready to listen to our sharing. We would be wasting our and God's energy to share with such a person except very minimally.

If a person's reaction to our sharing is anger, argument, or avoidance, we know that either the person needs more work on acceptance before she's ready to hear, or that we are perhaps over-zealous in our sharing. We need to learn patience when sharing, as in all things.

Sometimes we may spend an hour talking to one of our fellow parts of God, feeling that this person isn't hearing a word, but a week or a month or a year later, that person may come to us and thank us for that long talk that day, way back then. Or we may hear her say something later which we recognize may have come from our sharing.

Probably the most important aspect of sharing with other parts of God is that it doesn't matter whether we help the other person or not. What does matter is having the willingness to help and acting on that willingness by trying to help very gently. This has an extremely beneficial effect on us. We are the ones who are brought closer to our fellows by being willing to share and by sharing. Since what we share are all God's ideas, and God extends Himself to all of us equally, when we share our experience or spiritual attitudes with another, we are helped. We need only be sure that we let go of the results — let go of the importance we attach to whether we are helping or not. We just do the "footwork" and God does the rest. When we are truly sharing from the heart, we are sharing God, and God sees to it that the people we share with receive as much help as they are ready to accept. That is not our business; that is God's business. Our business is only to make ourselves available as channels to help those whom God puts in our path.

Chapter 15
Toward the Infinite

We have traveled a long way in this book and yet we have also stood still. Though we have mapped out the road for a transformation from ego-bound human to divine-like being, reading a book about the road is far different than traveling it. It may be a beginning — a tiny step toward our realization of the Higher Power within us.

One of the problems we encounter when traveling such a road is that though we're all heading toward the same place — awareness of our unity or Oneness with the Infinite God within us — we all start from different places. We all start from an ego space, but because of our social, cultural, national, regional, ancestral, and family environment differences, as well as our individual experiences in possible previous lives in the physical state, our egos manifest in a myriad different ways. For this reason, especially at the beginning of our journey, we travel what appear to be different roads. We are members of different religions, social classes, economic levels. Our skin color, body shapes, eye and hair color are different. We have gone through different birth, childhood, and adolescent experiences. Some of us were brought up by loving, caring, sensitive parents; others by parents who themselves have not learned how to express the love that is within them.

The list of our differences is endless. But one common thing we need to notice about these numerous differences is that they are all ego differences. They are all external differences. For this reason, it is difficult to predict what initial path any one of us will take toward our spiritual awakening. Some of us may come to an awareness of our inner Higher Power through great pain and struggle, and possibly near-death experiences; others may have been brought up in a spiritual atmosphere where the existence of a loving God was never questioned and His manifestation was always evident. These are fortunate indeed, but even some of them have probably gone through some difficult period because of their separation from God. Perhaps these souls accomplished in previous lifetimes what we have chosen to do in this one. One of the very helpful things we learn in this ego taming process is to stop comparing ourselves to anyone else. It is not their trip we need to take; it is our own.

Regardless of where we have been, after we travel the path of expanding awareness for a while, we realize that our outer differences don't matter and neither does the speed of our progress. The only really important thing is that we eventually become convinced *we* are the ones who are keeping ourselves from our serenity, our freedom, and our joy. We need to begin the work of removing the internal and mostly unconscious blocks our ego puts in our way.

We need to realize that, though other people can help us in doing this work, we have to do our own work. No one else can do it for us. And we need to take as long as we need to do it. As we do this work, we try to be aware of and minimize the extent to which our ego will resist and slow us down, even when it is under the guise of pushing to get it done and over with faster.

In contrast to the many ego differences I mentioned above, our egos are also similar in many ways. When we're on a spiritual path, the similarities are much more important than the differences. Our egos almost always make use of similar defenses. We need to learn what these are and to recognize them in order to let go of them and allow ourselves to change.

All of our egos harbor resentments from our past ego hurts and "defeats." Even if we have repressed them to the subconscious level, they're still there, affecting our present reactions. Letting these unconscious "unfeelings" from the past emerge is just part of the work we need to do as we continue our journey to God. We need to learn to see our everyday life experiences as opportunities for growth rather than as an endless series of events that beat us down. This is especially true of those experiences we have problems with. If we have a problem, it is *always* an unconscious, unfinished feeling within us that is causing it. The person whom our ego thinks is causing the problem is actually helping us to face whatever is within us that we need to look at. Recognition of this is one of the big differences between someone who has had a spiritual awakening and is on a spiritual path and someone who is not.

When we have a spiritual awakening, our outlook changes in many major ways — in fact, it reverses completely. Instead of seeing our cup as always half empty, we see it as half full or more. Instead of concentrating on our failings and shortcomings and how far we have yet to go, we begin to count our blessings and feel gratitude for the distance we have already traveled. We remember how we were and where we came from, and see how much we've improved and are still improving.

We begin to realize that we're engaged on a spiritual journey to God and put development of spiritual and emotional awareness first on our list of priorities. In that context, our problems and obstacles *all* become learning experiences from the most trivial to the gravest. We see how a traffic jam on the freeway or thruway can teach us patience rather than impatience. If we become physically ill, we see illness as a message from our body. Perhaps we need to learn to be quiet and search within ourselves for a new direction our life is to take. Instead of complaining and feeling self-pity, we see an opportunity to learn to be good to our body, to give it the rest and care it needs to heal. We honestly seek to know whether in our life before our illness we were too harsh on our body, not giving it enough sleep or the proper foods to maintain itself as a fit vehicle for our soul and our mind. Perhaps we went through long years of "burning the candle at both ends" to give our egos a sense of importance or to run away from the unresolved anger and resentments seething inside us.

Any catastrophe or loss, no matter how severe, can become a positive experience for growth, if we let it. This doesn't mean that we don't experience feelings of deep loss, grief, and emptiness for a time. It means that we allow ourselves all these feelings associated with loss, possibly including anger, fear, and guilt. In our own time and way, we let ourselves come to a resolution of these feelings within us and to a realization that our life is meant to continue, even though changed. Eventually, and this may be a few days or weeks to several years, depending on the magnitude of the loss and the degree of our attachment, we see that the experience of that loss has made us stronger and has contributed to the progress of our spiritual awakening, or perhaps even initiated it.

Our unsurrendered ego will always look at any loss as a terrible thing and will want to hang on to that view forever, feeling more and more depleted with each loss. But when we have a spiritual awakening, our ego surrenders to some degree, and we, our I, begin to see behind the immediate outward appearance that the ego sees. We allow ourselves to go through the grieving that we must do when our ego suffers a loss, and then go on to allow our new experience to unfold so we can continue our process of spiritual awakening.

When we spiritually awaken, our whole life changes from being hard and painful to becoming easier and happier, more pleasant and pain-free. We become less interested in selfish pursuits and more willing to help our fellow parts of God. Our attitude toward life changes from one of self-centeredness and greed, to one of serving humankind as best we know how. We become confident that God has an infinite supply — more than enough for every man, woman, child, animal, and plant He has made on this earth; and that He does provide for all equally when we let Him. We come to know that inequalities in the material world are caused by runaway egos which become fearful of loss, insufficiency, and thus make a world of material scarcity for some and over-abundance for others. In God's Kingdom, there is no lack, and the key to achieving the Kingdom on earth is the surrender of the ego.

As this process of spiritual awakening continues within us, we find that we grow in appreciation of the Higher Power within us and let Him increasingly guide our lives. We learn how to listen inwardly for this guidance on a daily or moment-to-moment basis. Whereas before we might have had a very low opinion of intuition, we realize more and more that Divine Guidance flows to us through our intuition to our growing consciousness.

We learn that a great deal of our growth takes place at the invisible, subconscious level — the level where many of our problems are hidden from us by our egos. This type of growth requires very little effort on our part. Instead of trying to *make* things happen, we learn to let the Divine Presence unfold, and to *let* things happen. Another way to say this is that when we try to make things happen, we're dealing at the level of ego and effects. When we let the Divine Presence unfold, we are aligning ourselves with the Cause which naturally and effortlessly brings about good results. To the ego, things just appear to happen.

Although at first we are awkward about this, we learn just how much "footwork" on our part is sufficient. Our compulsive bent toward over-control and over-activity diminishes. We get out of our own way. We stop stepping all over our own feet. We don't need to engage in ego battles or ego games anymore to try to get everyone to do our will. We realize there is a Will much more important than our ego's, and when we learn to attune ourselves to that Will, our lives straighten out. We become pleasant, loving, creative people who are here to serve by doing the Will of God within us rather than the will of our ego.

Further benefits resulting from our spiritual awakening are that our obsessions and compulsions are lifted from us. We stop manipulating ourselves and those close to us. We learn to let go and let God; live and let live. We try to be helpful to others because we see them more as they are — our fellow parts of God. Our prejudices against ethnic, social, or cultural groups slip away. We replace old feelings of "we against them" with "we're all here together, heading toward the same place, our Source, our Creator, God, because there is nowhere else to go." The only alternative to traveling toward God is increasing isolation, illness, madness, destruction, and death. We have been there; we know what that's like.

At times the road back gets very rocky. We stumble and fall. But with the help of our fellow parts of God, we pick ourselves up and continue. Though the road may become narrower as we go, it also becomes more joyous and even exhilarating if we allow it.

We find that as we become more centered within the Higher Power part of us, our ego becomes less real, less threatening, less compelling. We're able to go through more difficult learning experiences without the great fears or anxiety attacks we used to have. The closer we become identified with the Higher Power within us, the more willingly our ego surrenders and the more beautiful, calm, serene we and all those around us become. At times, it may seem as though our ego's surrender becomes harder rather than easier. That is because we're encountering more deeply entrenched ego beliefs. We're asking our ego to surrender in progressively more difficult areas, which we could not have tackled without the prior experience of the "easier" ones.

We increasingly adopt an attitude of giving rather than getting or taking, and we learn the joy of receiving humbly and graciously from our own giving. We no longer have to be only the giver and never the receiver (or vice-versa) because we no longer give to make our ego feel good. We now learn to give because that is the nature of God within us and we allow That Nature to express itself outwardly through us.

We learn that, because of the cyclical nature of our ego, our spiritual progress occurs in cycles. At times, our ego can take no more surrender. It rebels and takes charge again. We feel the effects of these "slips" or "setbacks" sooner and learn to recognize them as the low points in our ego cycle. We don't chastise ourselves or our egos for them. We know that each "low" will be followed by another "high" if we continue steadfastly on the path. The lows are as much a natural part of our journey as the highs. We cannot seem to have one without allowing the other. Cycles are a natural occurrence in the physical world. After rain comes sunshine, then more rain and more sunshine. The seasons repeat their endless cycles of birth, growth, blossoming, fading, death and rebirth, as the earth continues its circular journeys around the sun. It is that way with us as it is in all of nature. After togetherness comes distance; after anger and distance comes making up and coming closer again. The more we accept these cycles within us and rejoice in them instead of trying to make them what our ego wants them to be, the more serene we become.

We also learn that these cycles abate as time goes on, the lows are less low, come less often, and end sooner. The cyclical changes tend to smooth out as we approach the Higher Power because His Nature, unlike the ego's, is unchanging and steadily Higher. At the beginning, when we are nearly all ego, we are very often low and have very few highs. Some of us have lengthy depressions that seem to last forever. As our ego surrenders progressively more, and we more often find ourselves in the company of our Higher Power, our spirits soar, and our lows come back more rarely and depart rather quickly. If we continue this ego surrender process to its logical conclusion, we can expect eventually to reach the eternal bliss of God, which we find so hard to believe possible.

As we continue our spiritual journey, we realize more and more that we, our own ego and no one else, are responsible for anything negative that happens to us. There are no accidents or coincidences. If we become involved in an "accident," we come to know that at some unconscious level, we cooperated by placing ourselves at the time and place of the accident so that we might learn a lesson from it. When our ego is in control, we will likely not learn the lesson, and may have to repeat the accident or unconsciously set up a new one. The more our ego surrenders, the more open and willing we are to learn the spiritual lessons within each and every experience of our lives, whether our ego calls it good or bad. We realize more and more that this is what we're here for — to learn enough from our experience to reach the point where we become consciously reunited with God, our Father/Mother who created us.

In this context, the petty everyday occurrences of our lives which used to be such a chore and struggle begin to lose a lot of their punch. As we let go of them and increasingly turn them over to our Higher Power through our transforming "I," they seem to take care of themselves. As we rely more on the guidance of God within, our struggle gradually ceases. We realize we can let the temporal/material life happen to us while we devote a minimum of effort to living at that level, and free our energy to become more aware of the spiritual essence in each experience. This awareness becomes the joy of living because everything that brings us closer to God increases our enjoyment of life.

I hope I have made clear by this time that, though it often acts in abominable ways, the ego is not a villain or monster which must be smashed, killed, controlled, maimed, ignored, or even transcended. The ego is, after all, a part of ourselves which we need to operate in the physical, space/time world. It is an entity which we have made and maintained to fill the gap left by our apparent separation from God, our

Father/Mother and our Source. *We cannot kill the ego any more than we can kill or get rid of any part of ourselves.* The more we try to get rid of a part of us, the more we delude ourselves, as we have already seen, with unacceptable and unwanted emotions. Getting rid of things or making believe they aren't there is the ego's way. That's why it doesn't work. God's way, which is the way we adopt as we wake spiritually, is to allow, embrace, include, accept, to love and to create. So we must learn to accept and to love our ego. The love and grace of God expressed through our "I" is what transforms our mistaken and often crazed, obsessed, destructive ego to a tame, cooperative, willing part of us which functions effectively in the space/time world under the guidance of the loving God within us.

As we learn much needed patience, we realize we are engaged in a life-long growth process, and there is no hurry. We have all the time we need because God knows no time — only this holy instant — the Here and Now which is Eternity. So we learn to stop going through life kicking and screaming, as Hugh Prather says, and patiently begin to do the inner work that we need to find our Creator within us. And slowly we learn that this infinite, beautiful, bountiful, loving, giving Being has implanted all of Himself within each and everyone of us, and each and every creation down to the smallest grain of dust and particle of every atom. We begin to realize our inner beauty and the beauty of all around us. As our eyes see the outer beauty in the sky, the sunset, the hills, the forests, the oceans, and each other's faces and bodies, our soul contemplates the inner beauty without which the outer forms could not exist. We begin to see with our "inner eyes" that our all-loving Higher Power wants nothing but the best for all of us since we are all part of Him and that's what He must want for Himself. We realize that as long as we remain in the loving arms of our Father/Mother, we cannot fear because there is nothing to fear. Only our egos know fear because they invent it; and the ego fears only the things inside us which it still tries to hide from us.

As we continue on our path, more is revealed to us, and the more we begin to know — no matter how dimly at first — the more beautiful it all becomes until we eventually know that we are all truly parts of an Infinite God and therefore, Infinite ourselves. In our Infinity, we are all joined together. Finally, in our unity, we are healed and become whole.

Chapter 16
Becoming One

The search for unity is a very basic urge within us which is usually misunderstood by our egos. Our "I"'s realize that we are already all united within the One Higher Power which we are all a part of. Our "I"'s would like to live their lives in the physical environment in this state of unity. Unfortunately, they must do so through the medium of an ego which believes in separation for fear of being annihilated. The ego has the greatest difficulty understanding or practicing unity. Being split and divided within itself, torn by conflicts of all kinds which it sets up, it is almost impossible for it to conceive of harmonious unity with even one other person, let alone all humankind. Sensing vaguely that unity has something to do with love, the ego vainly tries to love, which as we have seen, is impossible. The ego is too fearful to love. So it searches endlessly for ways to love without giving up the control it uses to assuage its fears — another impossibility.

In its imagined search for love, the ego is constantly baffled because it doesn't realize the incompatibility of its goals which cause ongoing conflict. Because of its early conditioning in receiving attention and being cared for by others, especially mother, as a baby, the ego defines love as something it *must* have from someone else to be happy. Left alone, the ego experiences loneliness which it often equates with nothingness: I am alone; I am lonely, no one loves me; I'm not worth loving; I'm nothing." That is true. The ego by itself *is* nothing. It constantly avoids facing the all-too-horrible consequence of this truth by seeking other egos to focus on and longing for the one special ego it can form a lasting relationship with. The ego's hunger for this constant companionship and the acceptance, approval, and false sense of worth that it brings, is so great that it will sometimes take almost anyone who is willing to give it the pseudo-love it seeks or even just a little bit of it. The insane ego fails to know itself and to take into account compatibility factors, hidden purposes and motives, or other possible future stumbling blocks.

Two hungry egos meet, each looking to the other for its validation, fall madly "in love," which itself is a tremendous ego-validating process, and promptly proceed to mistake the intensity of their short-term, pseudo-love for long-term, truly loving compatibility. Most often today, the intensity of the immediate pseudo-love is made even stronger by immediate sexual involvement which invariably brings into play at too early a stage, emotional attachment and entanglement with resulting fears and resentments. Initially these fears and resentments take the form of "lovers' quarrels" but they are the result of two egos rushing headlong into relationships without pausing to examine "Who am I and who is this other person? How are we alike and how dissimilar?" Most of all, we need to ask what unresolved problems with resulting locked-in emotions do I have inside me left over from my childhood — especially my relationship with my mother or father, or both, and possibly with my brothers and sisters as well?

These unresolved emotional conflicts from our early relationships with the most significant people in our lives, more than anything else, are responsible for the break-up of relationships and marriages. It doesn't matter whether we're sixteen or seventy-six; if we haven't brought to consciousness and accepted in a very personal, direct way all the feelings we stuffed down as a child toward mother, father and sibling, these will come up to haunt us in our close relationships in an effort at resolution. This is often called unfinished business from the past. The feelings associated with this unfinished business stay repressed in our unconscious and act upon us in undesirable ways until we're ready to face them head-on. They "demand" to be heard, accepted and consciously released before we can have any peace.

We usually go about trying to resolve these unconscious, unexpressed feelings by unconsciously choosing a partner or mate who will unconsciously trigger those feelings within us and bring them to the surface where we can deal with them more directly. Since we're not aware of this unconscious process, our ego soon begins to feel really unhappy with our mate or partner for treating us in such a shabby way. We begin to find fault with him or her and a lot of the things he/she does or doesn't do. If we were once intensely "in love," we begin to see the "love" fade as our unresolved inner feelings surface and we blame our partner for causing them. *Our partner doesn't cause them any more than we cause his or hers. Each of us merely triggers in the other what is already slumbering within*, perhaps has been festering there for years, and needs to be brought to consciousness for resolution. This process of mutual triggering which the ego deplores so much and tries its best to ignore by blaming, is necessary for the growth of our soul. It is carried out under guidance of our "I." But if we're not aware of the underlying process behind the surface event, we remain under control of our ego. We become disenchanted, antagonistic, hostile, angry, and possibly rageful toward our partner and often ourselves as well. We fail to realize that most of those intense feelings are those of the little child we once were, toward one or both of our parents. On the surface, we may experience a sense of failure and worthlessness because we cannot please our partner, and a sense of righteous indignation because our partner doesn't please us.

Unless we realize the underlying process of the past, we focus only on the current situation and remain unaware that we're unconsciously projecting the characteristics of our parent(s) onto our partner. We also remain unaware that we may have chosen a partner who has a personality very similar to that of our parent. We either fight constantly, fall into depression or apathy, or run away from the relationship. If we run, we think we're getting away from the problem by getting away from our partner, but since the problem is inside us, we take it with us and recreate an almost identical situation with someone else in an attempt at resolution and growth. Sooner or later, we find there is no escape. We either meet the problem here and now, or we have to face it at another time in another place.

This is why many people run from one relationship or marriage to another choosing almost the same type of person each time. The ego looks upon this as endless punishment, but from the point of view of the soul, it's a repeated attempt to free itself from ego mistakes of the past. The soul, which includes the "I" and is of God, will not be denied. That is because God cannot be denied. He is all, everything, everywhere. He does and always will prevail. He is the One and only loving Power of creation and growth.

When we begin to see the unconscious replay of our childhood underlying our close relationships, and realize that we need to go through the feelings of the past in the present, we can begin to cooperate with the unfolding process rather than let our ego continue to fight it. We (I) can begin to separate current triggering feelings from the intense past feelings. We (I) can begin to see that much anger, resentment, and guilt we feel toward our partner is really displaced from our mother and/or father. We then begin to appreciate how angry we must have been as little children. We see that we may have hidden this anger from ourselves and everyone else at the time because it wasn't OK to be angry at mommy or daddy who were the people we depended on so much for love, approval and to tell us that we were OK individual people.

Very often that is the source of our unconscious anger; that our parents didn't treat us as worthy individuals. For whatever reasons related to their own ego limitations and unresolved frustrations, they may have treated us as their parents treated them — perhaps as second class citizens with little or no "rights," or as not entitled to feelings, but having to behave properly to fit in with the "norm." Perhaps they really loved us but were too ego-bound themselves to be able to show it or express it. Probably they didn't know that parents' prime function is to love their child. They mistakenly thought their prime function was to teach us manners or to be smart, ambitious, self-reliant or self-supporting, and that love came after, not before, all of these. Possibly they wanted to love us, and show us that they did, but had too many problems of their own to contend with. Perhaps they had never had the experience of being loved for themselves and as themselves.

Whatever the reasons, we come to realize that they did the best they could. By reliving the feelings of our past that we didn't allow ourselves to feel or express then, we slowly come to accept our childhood and our parents with all their "good" and "bad" aspects.

Many of us think we have already done this when we have barely begun. We say we had a good childhood. We can't remember anything really bad happening to us. Our mother may have been sick with a physical disability as long as we can remember, but we tell ourselves that we never suffered from that. Or perhaps, we had occasional wistful feelings about having a mother like other children, but it was nothing "serious."

Those of us who believe this way have not looked very far into our subconscious and have a lot of work ahead of us.

Most of us are ill-equipped as parents to deal with our children's feelings, to help them to feel them, good and bad. We either over-protect our children or disregard them and their feelings. When they hurt, we want to "make it all better" for them so they won't experience the hurt, won't feel the loss or sadness, instead of letting them cry when they need to and just standing by them and letting them know we love them while they do it.

Many of us parents are so intent on teaching our children to be "good" adults that we concentrate heavily on their behavior to the almost total exclusion of their feelings. We lay so many expectations on them regarding proper behavior, good grades in school, eating proper foods, keeping their rooms clean, that they become anxious, compulsive, and obsessive by the time they're six or seven. Others rebel against their parents' attempts to manage their lives, and become unruly and unmanageable "delinquents."

These child-parent interactions bring about strong unconscious feelings in most children which linger on into adulthood and tend to keep the child emotionally tied to the parent. It doesn't seem to matter whether the tie is one of docility and submission or open rebellion. Both are outward signs of dependency, and many of us oscillate between the two. The tie of resentment is just as strong as that of attraction and can only be broken by the child reliving as an adult any unresolved conflict toward the parent. If this isn't done through some form of therapy, it will crop up in any close relationship we may form and interfere with it. For the relationship to flourish, these unconscious emotional conflicts will need to be faced and released.

In some way, each of us will have to break the tie with the parent we were most attached to, whether through "love," hate, idol worship, fear, guilt or resentment. Often, we can't do this in a relationship. We need to be on our own for a while to establish a conscious contact with the Higher Power within us which eventually leads to a spiritual awakening.

To improve this conscious contact with God, as we understand Him, we need to come into conscious contact with more and more of our unconscious selves which our ego tries to keep hidden from us. We can do this through a process such as the one outlined in this book. As we continue this process, we slowly grow spiritually and emotionally, despite all our ego's efforts to stop us.

Little by little, we realize that every experience, good or bad, in our lives is an opportunity for learning the lessons we have come here to learn. If we can learn the lesson from each experience, there is no "bad" experience because all our experiences contribute to our growth which improves our lives. As we become more accepting of this process of growth, we stop fighting, kicking and screaming. We begin to see that our primary goal is not the material, social, cultural goals of the ego, but the spiritual and individual growth which brings us closer to the God within us — the God of the Universe — the One and only God.

As our ego becomes tamer and learns to surrender more easily, we become less hostile, less angry, and we learn to love. The love of the God within each of us comes through and expresses itself in our lives. We realize that the way to the inner peace we want so badly is by seeking to do God's loving will rather than follow the will of our ego. We're no longer afraid of the word or the attitude of humility. We seek more humbly to serve God by serving and helping our fellow human beings. We realize to an ever-greater degree that by serving God and our fellows, we really serve ourselves. Our whole attitude toward life changes from seeing only the negative and wallowing in it, to seeing the positive side of every experience — even the worst catastrophes. We progressively allow ourselves to feel more of our feelings as they rise up in us and find that, as we do this, we have an increasing ability to choose how to react, and how and when to express our feelings.

As we're increasingly freed from our inner conflicts, we become calmer, more serene, and more intuitive. We find that our intuition develops faster as we begin to appreciate its value and use it with more trust. We begin to live in the "now," the present moment, without constantly trying to change the past or fearfully anticipate the future. As our faith and trust in our Higher Power grows, we no longer have to believe that God is; WE KNOW. And we come to know that under our ego cover, we *are* God because He has given Himself to us. Our conviction of it becomes unshakable.

We no longer have to preach or put down God. We no longer have to recruit people to our way of life. We know that when everyone is ready, they find their way to the God within them. We're here to help those who want help and ask for it, and are willing to do the work required to receive the help. We know we can't do it for anyone else. We can only share what we have so that we may keep it, extend it, and thereby strengthen it in ourselves as well as those we share with. We know each of us walks alone, though we may walk hand in hand. We begin to want to share with our fellow parts of God as God shares Himself with all of us. In this sharing, we are all strengthened.

Slowly, as our attitudes continue to change, we begin to see that heaven can be here on earth. As we know more and more that the Kingdom of God is within us, and as we learn to let His loving energy express through us, we find that our external world becomes more serene, more loving, more free and joyous. Our ego slowly learns that our destination is the true, real, and only God. As it begins to accept this, it no longer needs to be God. We find that we can relax and enjoy the trip. We know and our ego learns that our Spirit already is God because there is only One Spirit and He IS God.

As we gradually realize that we're all going toward the God within, because that is the only place to go, we no longer need to fear that we will never get there. We know with increasing certainty that our Spirit is already there, and that our ego *is* getting there in its own time and its own way. We also know that in spirit, we have never left God — only our ego has. We become more accepting of those things within and outside us our ego still tries to control, and know that we're headed toward more joy as our ego learns to let go more completely. We learn that there is nothing to fear because God protects all those who are consciously and sincerely seeking to realize their unity with Him. We know too, that all we ever feared was what our ego kept hidden inside us, and unconsciously projected outward onto the world. When we face a fear and go through it with the help of God, it disappears. It no longer exists — if it ever did. Fear seems real only so long as we believe in it and in the power of our ego. As soon as we give that up and believe in only One Power, the Power of God, fear loses all its reality for us. Fear is only of the ego, and the greater the ego, the greater the fear. The more the ego surrenders, the more our fears dissolve. They are actually transformed by our "I" into positive energy for creative action.

Slowly we learn that emotional and spiritual growth for most of us is a life-long process. It is our only purpose for being here. It gives our life meaning.

We give up our old ideas that spiritual learning is based on the notion of intellectual education where we go to school for a few years, and then graduate. In spiritual growth, there is no graduation. Because God is infinite, the process has no end. It is as eternal as God is. God continually creates through us. As we realize that our place has always been with Him and in Him, we become co-creators. Paradoxically, as we depend more on God for support and sustenance, we become more responsible for ourselves and our growth. We begin to see that our responsibility lies not in *making* our growth happen or in pursuing it like an external goal, but in learning to be receptive to the energy of God — the Source of all energy — which naturally causes and enhances our growth, one day at a time. As we allow His energy to flow through us to an ever-increasing degree, learning becomes easier and faster. We don't have to suffer to learn as we used to in the beginning because our ego has become less resistant. We understand what is happening and we cooperate with the process.

As our intuition continues to open, we realize that we already have within us all the knowledge that God has, because God is within us. We find that this inner, intuitive knowledge requires no learning. We need only open ourselves to it inwardly and let it flow out. Doing this to an ever-greater degree becomes natural for us. We begin to place greater importance on this inner knowledge of God than we do on the outer knowledge of the world, because we see that knowing the inner knowledge makes learning the outer knowledge infinitely easier.

As we become more willing, more open to our own growth and change, the process of spiritual growth becomes one of joy, love and peace. We realize that life and spiritual growth are one and the same. When we learn to flow with the energy of God within us, we come to know that peace we have always yearned for — the peace that passes all understanding — the peace that fosters and sustains true love, and leads to unity and harmony through recognition of our eternal union and identity with the One and Only.

EPILOGUE

I hope this book has given you an inkling of a spiritual awakening as a process of individual transformation from ego-control to God-guidance; from ego-identity to identity with the Infinite Higher Power we're all a part of; from feeling like only a finite person in a flesh-and-bones body to realizing our Oneness with the Infinity of God and all the Universe; from placing almost exclusive emphasis on the material, time-bound world of things to realizing the primary, originating Source of Spirit which gives rise to everything material manifesting itself in a myriad variations of forms.

I hope also that this book has helped you appreciate that the process of transformation is a gradual one that proceeds naturally within us at its own pace if we merely open ourselves to it. It is not a process which can be rushed, pushed, or short-circuited. It cannot be *made* to happen. It can only be *allowed* to happen; and it does happen when our egos don't interfere with it or continue to resist it by hanging on to their blocks and defenses. We need not strive, push, or shove. We need only learn the patience to allow, to let, to encourage, and to invite. We need not get angry that we're not going faster. We need to learn to feel grateful and confident that we're progressing. We need continually to uncover more of the blocks within our unconscious egos as an archeologist slowly uncovers layer upon layer of civilization to unearth the hidden secrets of the past.

This is not a process we accomplish by taking a few courses and graduating. It is a lifetime project. For most of us, it may require numerous lifetimes. We need to remember that God's time is eternal. He will wait forever for all of us to return to the realization that we are One with Him and each other. He will also help us in any way He can without violating His own laws to tame our egos so we may realize Him more quickly.

You may say, "Well, since God is Infinite and all-powerful, why doesn't He just do it for us instead of waiting for us to do it?" I believe the answer is that He *is* doing it for us as much and as fast as our egos will allow. He has given everyone of us the same freedom of will as He has, and will not violate His laws by taking back what He has given. A gift of God is a gift of God forever. He does not give today and take back tomorrow unless we (our egos) don't believe we are worthy of keeping what He constantly gives us. We have turned our free will over to our egos so that our will is no longer free. Thus, we have set up separate housekeeping apart from the knowledge that we are part of God. Each of us, individually, is the only one who can assume responsibility for that separation and for the return realization journey as well.

It is an arduous journey because our egos don't let go easily. For most of us, the journey is too difficult to travel alone. We need the help of others who, like us, want to find a better way. As I mentioned before, one of the places to find this help is one or more of the "Anonymous" programs which use the Twelve Steps originated by Alcoholics Anonymous. The weekly meetings of these groups where people begin to come out of their ego isolation by sharing feelings at the "gut" level, are an important part of the growth process. Without such sharing it is difficult, if not impossible, for our egos to become honest enough to admit their insane ways. And without this admission, we remain locked in our ego's insanity until we become convinced there's no way out. When at that point, our ego surrenders, we find the way out; or the way out finds us.

If you can't attend meetings because there are none in your area, or because of physical problems, try to share by letter, phone, or tape recordings with members of these Twelve Step programs. The EHA (Emotional Health Anonymous) Central Office in Rosemead, California will put you in touch with members who want to share in this way. The people in these programs know they can only keep what they have been given by sharing it with others.

Whatever path you choose, make sure it has a heart. The way you know this is that it is a gentle path with love in it. The ego is very good at harshness, hostility, confrontation, attacking, deceiving, being deceived or seduced, controlling, being controlled, and thinking it knows the only way. But God is love, gentleness, patience, and He gives us the freedom to find our own way. He never tells us, "This is the way; you'd better do it or else . . ." He never judges, measures, criticizes, or in any way says, "You're not doing it right." If you find these things in your path, recognize them as ego tactics of a path which probably doesn't have a heart at its core, or perhaps only outwardly appears to have one. Individuals in any path will at times use these ego tactics because our egos are trained to do these things. They don't know anything else. We (our individual I) have to teach our ego slowly and gently that its surrender is the way to God and to peace, understanding, unity, love, freedom, and joy.

It has been fun sharing this book with you. At this moment, my ego doesn't know whether the book will be published and it's a little worried about it. But the Higher Power within me knows, and I'm learning to trust that Power more and believe in my ego's doubts and negative antics less. The more I realize that my ego's fears, resentments, greeds, or anything else negative that it cooks up are not real and are only temporary, the more at ease I feel, and the more trusting and confident I become that these negative ego inventions need no longer rule my life. The more firmly I believe this consciously and unconsciously, the more it is manifested in my outer and inner experience. At the same time, the spiritual reality of God emerges as the Only Reality. I become aware that my ego's existence in its present state is sustained only by my and other egos' belief in it.

I realize that I know only a little, but the little I have learned since I began my conscious spiritual transformation process over 18 years ago, makes sense and fits together. Before that time, nothing seemed to make much sense because it was all ego insanity. I believe there are no great or small mysteries. There is only knowledge we have yet to learn or remember that we already know. As we begin to come out of our ego shell, this knowledge is revealed to us to use on our journey and to share with others who feel ready to hear and use it.

If you have read this far in this book, you're apparently ready to hear what I've learned. Many have traveled far beyond us. Much of what I hear and read of what they share does not yet make sense to me. I accept that at some future time, it will make sense as I continue the journey. At that time, it will probably blend in with what is revealed through my own intuition, as the knowledge in this book blends in with other spiritual works.

I believe this book was written mostly by the Higher Power within me which I'm a part of. My ego could not have written it. It would still be on Page One trying to figure out exactly the right words and grammar, and worrying about getting the punctuation perfect. The words on these pages came with a flow and ease which can only come from the Higher Power within us. They seemed to give me a great deal of joy as they flowed out of me. My ego tried its usual delaying functions of procrastinating, criticizing, downgrading and doubting. At times, it became impatient and wanted to rush to the point of obsession, putting aside all other pursuits to "get this book done!" But throughout the writing period which lasted more than three years, I practiced listening to the inner guidance of my Higher Power rather than giving in to my ego's tactics. I recognized my ego at work and accepted its antics but found that *I* could make a choice. Most of the time, I chose my Higher Power's guidance.

I hope you will share your feelings, thoughts and ideas with me about this book. We can only learn and grow if we teach each other, even though we usually teach what we need to learn. So I would like to learn from you by way of your comments or questions. If anything in this book is unclear for you, your asking me about it will help me clarify it for both of us, and will help me write the next book. I will try to answer all of your letters that I can. By sharing with each other, we will both experience a greater sense of our unity in God. You may write to me in care of the publisher or directly at P.O. Box 452, Van Nuys, CA 91408, U.S.A. Until I hear from you, or hopefully meet some of you in person, may you let your Higher Power express "Hierself" through you, and through that expression may you find increasing peace, love, and happiness.

From the material, lead us to the Spirit,
From separation, lead us to Oneness,
From ego, lead us to God.

— Adaptation of Sanskrit Prayer

APPENDIX
Some General Guidelines on Choosing a Therapist

Choosing a therapist can be a difficult and confusing business. Perhaps that is one reason people wait so long to see one even when they really need to. More important reasons may be that our ego-oriented society still tends to minimize or deny emotional problems. If they do exist, we're expected to be able to handle them by ourselves. Even with the greatly increased emphasis on the human psyche during the last fifty years, there still seems to be in the minds of many people a considerable stigma associated with emotional or mental problems. There also seems to be a good deal of confusion among us about what kinds of therapists are available, and what similarities and differences exist among them.

This brief appendix cannot be an exhaustive guide to choosing a therapist. Rather, it is an assemblage of my limited knowledge and opinions. It's clear that I haven't done a scholarly study on the subject. Rather, I've written down what I know and believe about it in an attempt to help you make a start toward your own search for the "right" therapist for you, should you choose to consult one. As such, the following information is not meant to be totally objective, but rather reflects my own personal views and biases.

The most confusing factor for most people attempting to select a therapist is that there are so many different "schools" or systems of therapy to choose from. The safest and probably most productive way to start is to avoid a therapist who is rigidly locked into a particular system such as Transactional Analysis (T.A.), Gestalt Therapy, or Psychoanalysis, to the exclusion of all others. By nature, systems are limited, and they are often applied in a relatively structured way which can be limiting to clients. Systems are usually invented or discovered by one person, and embellished and broadened by his/her disciples (T.A. — Erich Berne; Gestalt — Fritz Perls; and Psychoanalysis — Sigmund Freud, for example). Most systems of this type are closed-ended, meaning that they don't allow for continued growth of the individual, especially in a spiritual direction.

Such relatively closed-ended systems may be an OK place to start for many people, and may be helpful in the initial stages of self-exploration, but they are limited in what they can accomplish in a long-term, transformational sense. One of their limitations comes from the fact that such systems are invariably based on theoretical frameworks which arise out of incomplete, at least partially ego-defined knowledge of the human psyche. Another is that proponents of such systems, in their efforts to prove that their system is the best, often attempt to make their system appear to be the universal answer. Then, they try to fit all people into their limited frameworks. In so doing, they tend to ignore those client experiences which their particular system doesn't account for, or to distort those experiences to the point where they will fit into their theoretical frameworks.

To be fully validated, and therefore most enhancing to the client's growth, all of his/her experiences, beliefs, attitudes, and values must be viewed with as little distortion as possible, whether or not the therapist's system accounts for them. A therapist committed to a system may have difficulty doing this.

This doesn't mean that if you go to a therapist who is oriented toward a particular system you will get bad therapy. It does mean that if you choose a therapist who is eclectic, you will be less likely to be viewed in a limiting or restricting way. An eclectic therapist is familiar with all systems, and combines the best from several or all of them in accordance with the client's needs as they change throughout the course of therapy.

Many therapy systems are ego-oriented, seeking to strengthen what is believed to be a weak ego. The tremendous ego strength required by a person to stay in a depression and barely functioning at the ego level is usually unrecognized. It is negative and often unconscious ego strength, to be sure, but it is far from weakness of the ego. It is precisely such a strong ego, gone completely out of control through its own attempts at over-control that can bring us to the point of near-physical death. The ego, if left to its own devices, will always end up attempting to kill us despite its best intentions to save us.

The type of therapy which best represents the view of the human psyche described in this book is Transpersonal Psychotherapy which is based on Transpersonal Psychology. This system — if it can be called that — is open-ended. It recognizes the infinite, spiritual power and essence existing within each of us and accepts the ego as the greatest barrier to the expression of that Power in ourselves and our lives.* Humanistic Psychology is a close second. Some humanistic psychologists are also transpersonal, but not all.

Even more important than system orientation, look for sincere warmth, empathy, understanding, and support from your therapist — not to the point where it is overdone and manipulative, thus catering too much to your ego

---

* If you would like a list of transpersonally oriented therapists, write to the Association for Transpersonal Psychology, P.O. Box 3049, Stanford, California 94305. For a small fee, they will send you a world-wide directory of such therapists. Their directory is not a complete list since it includes only those who are members of the Association.

needs, but rather to where you're treated with dignity and seen as a potentially capable person who may have temporarily gone off the path and lost his/her way.

Believe it or not in this day and age, there are still some therapists who believe that sexual intercourse with their clients is the best way to help them work through sexual inhibitions. If your therapist makes *any* sexual overtures whatsoever, no matter how much he or she thinks this will help your progress in therapy, stop seeing that person immediately. The vast majority of the therapeutic community is strongly opposed to this practice and considers it not only unethical but potentially dangerous to the mental health of the client. I'm referring here to actual physical overtures or to verbally attempting to influence you toward physical sexual activities. It is of course perfectly ethical and usually necessary to discuss and explore verbally a client's sexual attitudes, beliefs, and mores since these may form an important part of the therapy. But it is not accepted practice for any therapist to engage in physical sexual activity with a client. If you feel able, I encourage you to report any such attempts to the appropriate professional associations.

The one exception to this rule is the use of the services of a professional sex surrogate, which should be done only when special circumstances warrant it. Any course of sex therapy with a professional surrogate should be undertaken only under supervision by a licensed therapist who does *not* engage in sexual relations with the client. Of course, the therapist is not present during the sessions with the surrogate which are conducted in absolute privacy. But during the course of this type of sex therapy, the client is seen by the licensed therapist and the professional surrogate in separate sessions. The therapist and the surrogate also communicate regularly between client visits regarding the progress of the therapy.

Choosing a therapist may seem like somewhat risky business, but then, so is going to a doctor or dentist, buying a car, or life itself, for that matter. To reduce the risk, you need to assure yourself that your therapist has had the proper training as evidenced by a Master's, Ph.D., or M.D. degree from a recognized or accredited college or university, and a valid license in those states where licenses are required. An exception to this is a paraprofessional therapist working under supervision of a licensed therapist. If your funds are limited, there are an increasing number of paraprofessional counseling centers which use a sliding scale to determine the fee based on the client's ability to pay. These centers train lay people to be counselors and eventually psychotherapists. Under competent supervision, paraprofessional therapists can become every bit as good as a professional person. Some professional centers also charge on a sliding scale.

It is also extremely important that your therapist, whether professional or paraprofessional, should have gone through a minimum of one year, but prefably two to three years of therapy with one therapist. He or she may have had additional therapy with other therapists, but at least one to three years with a single therapist. This may sound strange because we are so used to thinking of therapists as well, and ourselves as the sick ones who must go to a therapist for help. But there isn't a person alive who doesn't have some unresolved conflicts from the past, or some parts of himself his ego is unconsciously hiding from himself. To be truly helpful, a therapist must uncover and resolve these so they will not interfere in relationships with clients. Going through her own therapy is also the only way a therapist can understand the process of therapy in all its phases and ramifications, and the only way a therapist can come close to knowing what the client is experiencing as he goes through his own process of growth.

Unfortunately, there is no legal or professional requirement at present — at least in California, and to my knowledge, in the rest of the nation as well — for a licensed therapist to have gone through therapy.* Yet to me, this seems one of the most crucial requisites for doing effective therapy. I strongly urge you to consider your potential therapist on this basis, and to ascertain how much professional therapy he or she has had, when, and with whom.

Whether to choose a therapist with a Master's degree (e.g. M.A., M.S., or M.S.W.) or a Ph.D. or an M.D. degree often seems paramount to many people. The same question put another way is: "Should I go to a counselor, therapist, psychologist, or psychiatrist for my therapy?" Related to this question are the matters of fees, insurance reimbursement, and financial ability. Although pertinent, these questions seem to me less important than the issues of a therapist's orientation, personal feeling about himself and others, and whether he has had his own therapy.

In general, however, therapists with Master's degrees tend to be called counselors or therapists, those with Ph.D. degrees in psychology or a related field are usually called psychologists, and those with an M.D. degree are called psychiatrists. In California, Marriage, Family and

---

* *The only exception to this lack that I'm aware of is for psychoanalysts who, to be accredited by their professional associations, must have gone through a successful psychoanalysis with a senior psychoanalyst.*

Child Counselor (MFCC) is one designation for a therapist licensed by the State. To be licensed in the state of California, such a therapist must have a Master's degree in an appropriate field from an accredited college or university approved by the state, and must meet certain experience requirements including 3,000 hours of counseling-related experience, of which at least 2,000 hours must be direct, face-to-face, one-to-one, counseling of clients. Having completed the degree and the experience hours, the applicant therapist must then pass written and oral examinations given semi-annually by the State. The requirements set forth by the State to be licensed as a psychologist are similar except that the degree must be a Ph.D. or equivalent in psychology or a related field.

Psychiatry is considered a branch of specialization within the general field of medicine. A psychiatrist, therefore, begins training by completing a course of study leading to the degree of Doctor of Medicine or M.D. The doctor may then choose to specialize in psychiatry. This generally requires two additional years of study and one or two years of internship in a psychiatric hospital or ward. Being doctors of medicine, psychiatrists are qualified to prescribe medication whereas psychologists and counselors/therapists are not. Because of their clinical internship, psychiatrists may also be better equipped to treat patients with psychotic disorders. Psychologists may or may not be so equipped. Though many counselors or therapists may be prepared to work with people having occasional psychotic episodes, they are in general much more competent with clients who have the more common neurotic disorders, adjustment problems, or other ego-distortion problems.

In general, fees charged increase with the level of the degree because the amount of formal training and the time and money spent getting it increase correspondingly. For reasons stated above, it does not necessarily follow that a higher degree and greater formal training of the therapist result in higher quality therapy for the client. Therapist qualities of warmth, sincerity, integrity, empathy, self-awareness, and compassionate regard toward clients seem to be more important. These qualities arise more from a therapist's in-depth knowledge of herself, often gained through her own psychotherapy, than they do from formal academic training. In fact, too much academic training, if obtained at the expense of heart-felt, compassionate experience, can interfere with a therapist's competence.

In Southern California, counselor or therapist fees in 1985 range between $40 and $65 per hour; psychologist fees between $50 and $75 per hour; and psychiatrist fees between $65 and $100 or more. A therapy "hour" is usually 45 or 50 minutes to allow for re-centering or telephone calls between sessions. Some therapists of all types may see some clients for much less than these fees under certain circumstances or for charitable reasons.

Another question which often comes up is: "Do I need a male or female therapist?" The answer to this question is not nearly so important as it may appear. For most people, it doesn't seem to matter whether their therapist is a man or woman. Most therapists are aware that their personalities contain some characteristics that are considered "male" and some considered "female." Although a man usually has more male traits than female ones, and vice-versa, we are all androgynous in varying proportions. One purpose of therapy is to help us get in touch with and accept opposite-sex parts of ourselves that our egos may be unconsciously rejecting so that we may become more whole human beings. A good therapist who is open to both components within himself can help us do this, whether he/she is a man or woman.

One exception to this "it-doesn't matter" rule occurs when a client has had a traumatic childhood relationship with a person of one sex (usually mother or father) to the point where she has difficulty trusting someone of that sex. If the difficulty isn't too great, it may be worthwhile for a client to find a therapist of that sex to work through leftover feelings from childhood which will invariably come up during the therapy. If the difficulty in trusting is too great, it may be impossible for a client to establish enough trust with a therapist of the same sex as the parent or person he had the traumatic relationship with. There may be too much pent-up anger, resentment, and hostility even to begin to work on it constructively. In that event, a client would do well to choose a therapist of the other sex at the beginning, and perhaps change at a later time when a sense of self has been solidified and some of the anger has been worked through.

This is only a brief guide to choosing a therapist. Much more could be said. Beyond these general guidelines, there will still remain a certain amount of uncertainty and therefore risk. This will require faith and some trust on your part that the Higher Power within you, who knows all and has infinite wisdom, will guide you to the right therapist for you. During your selection process, it may be helpful to your ego to know that it is *not* like looking for a needle in a haystack. Many therapists are available who can be helpful to you, and only a few can be potentially harmful. Whether you believe it or not at this point, your Higher Power does provide an infallible, built-in protection which will always be effective if your ego allows it.

One more thing needs to be said. If your therapy seems to take longer than your ego thinks it should, the fault may not be with the therapist as your ego tries to tell you. Our egos are generally tougher and more resistant than we think or would like them to be. Part of the ego surrender process is accepting and going through what we need to go through. After thirty years of self-development, a great source of amazement to me is still that my own "basic training" in therapy took more than six years with a highly qualified and competent therapist. During the first three years, I seriously doubted his competence since my ego was telling me that I should be "cured" in no more than two to three years. Although I now usually accept it, I'm still amazed that my ego was as strong and obstinate as it was. Looking back on it from this vantage point, I remember that I had to start from scratch in 1955 when seeing a therapist was still considered a sign of sure insanity and a subject for much bad humor. Also, I had a very negative concept of anything spiritual at the time, and wanted to hear nothing about God or any kind of Higher Power. Had my ego been able to accept that it was not king or supreme ruler, and had it allowed for some belief in a constructive Higher Power, I believe my therapy would have been much shorter. I had to go through a long trust-building process with a kind, compassionate, and almost infinitely patient man before my ego was even willing to consider beginning to trust a spiritual Power greater than itself.

When all has been said and done about choosing a therapist, one of the best criteria may still be a recommendation from a friend whom you feel, and can see, has been helped by the therapist he or she has been seeing.

*   *   *

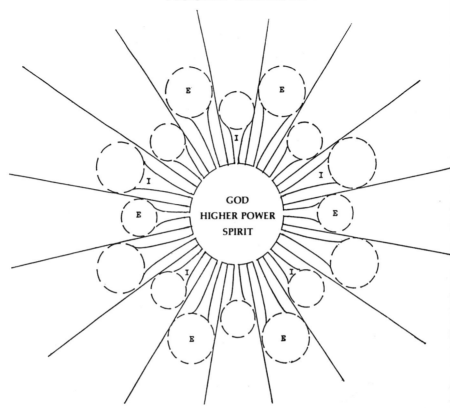

V-1
Higher Power, I's and Egos

The center circle represents the Higher Power, or God or Spirit. Since God extends to infinity in all directions, the rays branching out from the inner circle represent that extension — all-pervasiveness, omnipresence. The broadening "connectors" radiating out from the center are the individual "I's." They are the true "I" in each of us — the individual expression of the Higher Power within us. The picture shows our eternal connection with the Higher Power within. The "I's" terminate in our egos, represented on the chart by the small dashed circles. The circles are dashed because our egos are not real. But, to the extent that we believe they are, they prevent the further growth and extension of our "I." Various egos are at various distances from the Center, and the further "away" they are, the bigger and more controlling they are.

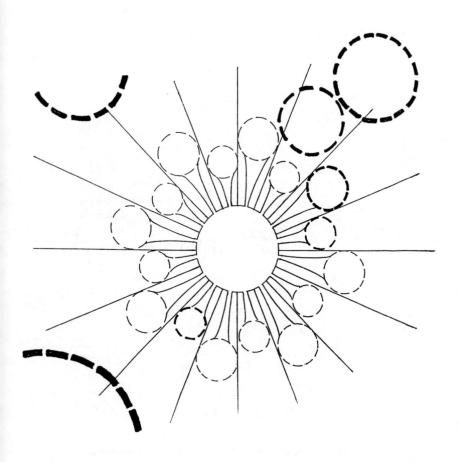

V-2 Ego Barriers

The chart shows that the further away from the Higher Power the ego
has wandered, the larger it becomes and the thicker are the barriers it
builds around itself for protection and isolation from other egos. These
farther egos are connected to the Higher Power by a thin line "I" rather
than the strong, thick "I" of the closer-in egos. This "I" of the furthest
egos has little chance to operate at the conscious level. It must let the ego
exhaust its own-will resources until it reaches the point where it becomes
willing to surrender. This process may entail a lot of pain and suffering
caused by the ego's insistence on using its own will — doing "it" all by
itself.

V-3 Surrendering Ego/Expanding I

As egos begin to surrender, the "I's" expand to their full potential which
is as infinite as God is. Each of us has the potential of becoming One
with God, or One God. At the top, the ego has surrendered to some
degree and the "I" is slightly expanded. Going counterclockwise around
the Center, depicts further stages of surrender with the ego becoming
smaller and simultaneously moving closer to God. The "I" progressively
expands. At the right side of the chart, the gradual surrender process is
shown in four stages of ego shrinkage and "I" expansion.

V-4 Ultimate State

This chart shows the Ultimate State of ego surrender and "I" expansion.
God's flower is in full bloom. All "I's" are fully expanded and merging
into each other forming One Unified Whole. Egos, which are a necessity
for those of us still inhabiting bodies, are at their maximum stage of
surrender (minimum size). All egos have become completely willing to
align their own will with the will and intentions of the Higher Power.
Egos function only as cooperative, willing intermediaries between the
One Spirit and individual bodies. Of course, individuality is maintained
within the Whole since each "I" becomes more fully "I-Self" during the
ego surrender process. Each "I" grows to its full, infinite potential and
becomes a free part of the Loving, Complete Oneness. In a color chart,
the individuality would be identified by a separate and distinct color for
each "I."

Suggestions for Further Reading

Anonymous, *A Course in Miracles*, Tiburon, California: The Foundation for Inner Peace, 1975.

Anonymous, *The Twelve Steps for Everyone . . . who really wants them*, Minneapolis, Minnesota: CompCare Publications, 1977.

Assagioli. R. *Psychosynthesis*, New York: The Viking Press, 1971. (Originally published in 1965)

_____ *The Act of Will*, New York: The Viking Press, 1973.

Bailey, A. *From Intellect to Intuition*, New York: Lucis Publishing Company, 1932.

_____ *Consciousness of the Atom*, New York: Lucis Publishing Company, 1922.

Benson, H. *The Relaxation Response*, New York: William Morrow and Company, Inc., 1975.

Bozarth-Campbell, A. *Life is Goodbye, Life is Hello, Minneapolis, Minnesota: CompCare Publications, 1982.*

Castaneda, C. *Journey to Ixtlan*, New York: Simon and Schuster, Inc., 1972.

_____ *Tales of Power,* New York: Simon and Schuster, Inc., 1974.

Goldsmith, J. *The Thunder of Silence,* New York: Harper & Row Publishers, 1961.

_____ *Practicing the Presence,* New York: Harper & Row Publishers, 1958.

Holmes, E. *The Science of Mind,* New York, New York: Dodd, Mead & Company, 1938. 35th Edition of the Revised and Enlarged Form.

James, W. *The Varieties of Religious Experience,* New York: Collier Books, 1961.

Jampolsky, G. G. *Love is Letting Go of Fear,* Millbrae, California: Celestial Arts, 1979.

Johnson, R. A. *He: Understanding Masculine Psychology,* New York: Harper & Row Publishers, 1974.

_____ *She: Understanding Feminine Psychology,* New York: Harper & Row Publishers, 1976.

Jung, C. G. *Mysterium Conjunctionis,* Princeton, N.J.: Princeton University Press, Bollingen Series XX, Vol. 14, 1963.

_____ *The Archetypes and the Collective Unconscious,* Princeton, N.J.: Princeton University Press, Bollingen Series XX, Vol. 9, Part 1, 1969.

_____*Symbols of Transformation*, Princeton, N.J.: Princeton University Press, Bollingen Series, Vol. 5, 2nd ed., 1970.

Kopp. S.B. *If You Meet the Buddha on the Road, Kill Him*, Palo Alto, California: Science and Behavior Books, Inc. 1972.

Lair, J.K. *I Don't Know Where I'm Going but I Sure Ain't Lost*, Garden City, N.Y.: Doubleday & Company, Inc., 1981.

_____*I Ain't Much, Baby — But I'm All I've Got*, Garden City, N.Y.: Doubleday & Company, Inc., 1972.

Monroe, R.A. *Journeys Out of the Body*, Garden City, N.Y.: Doubleday & Company, Inc. 1971.

Montgomery, R. *Here and Hereafter*, New York: Fawcett Crest Books, 1968.

_____ *The World Before*, New York: Fawcett Crest Books, 1976.

Roberts, J. *Seth Speaks*, Englewood Cliffs, N.J.: Prentice-Hall, 1972.

_____ *The Nature of Personal Reality*, Englewood Cliffs, N.J.: Prentice-Hall, 1974.

Singer, J. *Androgyny*, Garden City, N.Y.: Anchor Press/Doubleday, 1976.

Spaulding, B.T. *Life and Teaching of the Masters of the Far East*, Vol. 1 through 5, Marina Del Rey, California: De Vorss & Co., 1924.

Steinbrecher, E.C. *The Inner Guide Meditation*, Santa Fe, N.M.: Blue Feather Press, 1978.

Sugrue, T. *There is a River — The Story of Edgar Cayce*, New York: Holt, Rinehart & Winston, Inc. 1942.

Tart, C.T. *States of Consciousness*, New York: E.P. Dutton, 1975.

Troward, T. *The Hidden Power*, New York: Dodd, Mead & Company, 1921.

Wilber, K. *The Spectrum of Consciousness*, Wheaton, Ill.: The Theosophical Publishing House, 1977.

Till we meet or meet again,

May you let the Light of God
shine forth on your ego,
for that will heal it, tame it,
and help it learn to live by
the only Truth there is —
the Truth of God.